TRAVERSE
THEATRE

Traverse Theatre Company
in association with the Royal National Theatre Studio

Gagarin Way
by Gregory Burke

cast in order of appearance

Eddie	Michael Nardone
Tom	Michael Moreland
Gary	Billy McElhaney
Frank	Maurice Roëves
director	John Tiffany
designer	Neil Warmington
lighting designer	Chahine Yavroyan
composer	Mick Slaven
fight director	Terry King
stage manager	Gavin Harding
deputy stage manager	Brendan Graham
assistant stage manager	Kirsty Paxton
wardrobe supervisor	Anna Lau and Alison Brown
wardrobe assistant	Stephanie Thorburn
sound operator	Maria Bechaalani

**First performed at the Traverse Theatre
Thursday 12 July 2001, transferring to the Cottesloe Theatre
at the Royal National Theatre in September 2001**

TRAVERSE THEATRE

One of the most important theatres in Britain The Observer

Edinburgh's Traverse Theatre is Scotland's new writing theatre, with a 37 year record of excellence. With quality, award-winning productions and programming, the Traverse receives accolades at home and abroad from audiences and critics alike.

The Traverse has an unrivalled reputation for producing contemporary theatre of the highest quality, invention and energy, commissioning and supporting writers from Scotland and around the world and facilitating numerous script development workshops, rehearsed readings and public writing workshops. The Traverse aims to produce several major new theatre productions plus a Scottish touring production each year. It is unique in Scotland in its exclusive dedication to new writing, providing the infrastructure, professional support and expertise to ensure the development of a sustainable and relevant theatre culture for Scotland and the UK.

Traverse Theatre Company productions have been seen world wide including London, Toronto, Budapest and New York. Recent touring successes in Scotland include PERFECT DAYS by Liz Lochhead, PASSING PLACES by Stephen Greenhorn, AMONG UNBROKEN HEARTS by Henry Adam, HIGHLAND SHORTS, HERITAGE by Nicola McCartney and LAZYBED by Iain Crichton Smith. AMONG UNBROKEN HEARTS tranferred to the Bush Theatre, London in March 2001. PERFECT DAYS also played the Vaudeville Theatre in London's West End in 1999. In 2000 the Traverse co-produced Michel Tremblay's SOLEMN MASS FOR A FULL MOON IN SUMMER with London's Barbican Centre, with performances in both Edinburgh and London, and two world permieres as part of the Edinburgh Festival Fringe: SHETLAND SAGA by Sue Glover and ABANDONMENT by Kate Atkinson. For Festival 2001 the Traverse is also producing Iain Heggie's new play WIPING MY MOTHERS ARSE.

During the Edinburgh Festival the Traverse is one of the most important venues with world class premieres playing daily in the two theatre spaces. The Traverse regularly wins awards at the Edinburgh Festival Fringe, including recent Scotsman Fringe Firsts for Traverse productions KILL THE OLD TORTURE THEIR YOUNG by David Harrower and PERFECT DAYS by Liz Lochhead.

An essential element of the Traverse Company's activities takes place within the educational sector, concentrating on the process of playwriting for young people. The Traverse flagship education project CLASS ACT offers young people in schools the opportunity to work with theatre professionals and see their work performed on the Traverse stage. In addition the Traverse Young Writers group, led by professional playwrights, has been running for over three years and meets weekly.

ROYAL NATIONAL THEATRE STUDIO

GAGARIN WAY is part of SPRINGBOARDS - a series of partnerships created by the Royal National Theatre Studio with other theatres, enabling work by emerging writers to reach a wider audience.

The Studio is the National's laboratory for research and development providing a workspace outside the confines of the rehearsal room and stage where artists can experiment and develop their skills.

As part of its training for artists there is an on-going programme of classes, workshops, seminars, courses and masterclasses. Residencies have also been held in Edinburgh, Vilnius, Belfast and South Africa thus enabling artists from a wider community to share and exchange experiences.

Central to the Studio's work is a commitment to new writing. The development and support of writers is demonstrated through play readings, workshops, short-term attachments, bursaries and sessions with senior writers. Work developed there continually reaches audiences throughout the country and overseas, on radio, film and television as well as at the National and other theatres. Most recently work includes the award winning plays FURTHER THAN THE FURTHEST THING by Zinnie Harris, (Tron, Traverse, RNT) and THE WAITING ROOM by Tanika Gupta (RNT), THE WALLS by Colin Teevan (RNT), ACCOMPLICES by Simon Bent, MR ENGLAND by Richard Bean (in association with Sheffield Theatres) and THE SLIGHT WITCH by Paul Lucas (in association with Birmingham Rep) as well as a season of five new plays from around the world with the Gate Theatre. In addition to GAGARIN WAY, the Studio will be co-presenting MISSING REEL by Toby Jones at the Traverse during the Edinburgh Festival 2001.

FOR THE ROYAL NATIONAL THEATRE STUDIO

Head of Studio	Sue Higginson
Studio Manager	Matt Strevens
Technical Manager	Eddie Keogh
Studio Administrator	Chris Botterill
Press Representative	Lucinda Morrison

GREGORY BURKE

Gregory Burke was born in Dunfermline in 1968. After school and having dropped out of Stirling University he fulfilled a variety of vital roles in the minimum wage economy. GAGARIN WAY is his first play.

PREFACE

I wanted to write something about the Twentieth Century. That's usually how I begin an explanation of what I wanted to achieve when writing this play. It's not very helpful I know, but when I wrote the play it was the only century I had managed to live in. (Obviously, now, I feel like a weight has come off.) I also wanted to write a play about economics, it being the dominant (only?) theme in modern politics, and the source of real power in our increasingly globalised times. And finally, I wanted to write about men and our infinite capacity for self-delusion. So I wrote GAGARIN WAY.

The play is named after a street in the village of Lumphinnans in west Fife which was a hotbed of communism. As part of the Fife coalfield, its existence, and that of the towns and villages which surround it, was due solely to its proximity to coal. I moved to west Fife in 1984 and The Miners' Strike was in full flow. Fife was, of course, a very staunch and committed region during the dispute, even though everyone, including the miners, knew that they were, eventually, going to be beaten. (Coal was cheaper in Poland after all.) However inevitable defeat was not something that was ever going to break the strike and the vast majority of miners and their families endured to the bitter end. The mines closed, the ex-miners were swallowed up by the electronics factories and service industries which followed (attracted by government subsidy to areas of high unemployment) as were the dockyard workers at Rosyth, when the defence industries were decimated when the West celebrated the end of the Cold War. (Russia couldn't afford the arms race.) Economics decides the fate of people, not their politicians. Governments are powerless when up against a multi-national, the vagaries of the stock market and history. But the people remain. That's the constant. We remain and we find other things to keep ourselves amused.

I wanted to write something about the twentieth century and I wanted to write something about economics and I wanted to write about men and it turned into Gagarin Way. A comedy. I didn't expect it to be a comedy but when you consider the themes which emerged while I wrote it - Marxist and Hegelian theories of history, anarchism, psychopathology, existentialism, mental illness, political terrorism, nihilism, globalisation and the crisis in masculinity - then it couldn't really be anything else.

Gregory Burke
June 2001

BIOGRAPHIES

Terry King (fight director): Work for the Royal National Theatre: FOOL FOR LOVE, THE MURDERERS (Peter Gill), KING LEAR, THE SEA, OTHELLO, THE BIRTHDAY PARTY (Sam Mendes), CAROUSEL, THE CRIPPLE OF INISHMAN (Nick Hytner), THE RIOT (Mike Shepard), CHIPS WITH EVERYTHING, BATTLE ROYAL (Howard Davies), LONDON CUCKOLDS (Terry Johnson), WAITING FOR GODOT, TING TANG MINE (Michael Rudman), THREE MEN ON A HORSE, JOCOBOWSKI AND THE COLONEL (Jonothon Lynne), THE HOMECOMING (Roger Michelle). For the RSC: TROILUS AND CRESSIDA, RICHARD III (Sam Mendes), ROMEO AND JULIET, CYMBELINE (Adrian Noble), PERICLES, JULIUS CEASAR, CORIOLANUS (David Thacker), HENRY V, HAMLET (Matthew Warchus), A PATRIOT FOR ME (Peter Gill), THE WHITE DEVIL (Gael Edwards), COMEDY OF ERRORS, TWELFTH NIGHT (Ian Judge), OTHELLO, HENRY IV PARTS 1 & 2 (Michael Attenborough), BITE OF THE NIGHT (Danny Boyle), SINGER (Terry Hands), A MIDSUMMER NIGHT'S DREAM, THE BROKEN HEART, ROMEO AND JULIET (Michael Boyd), AS YOU LIKE IT, MACBETH (Greg Doran). For the Royal Court: OUR COUNTRY'S GOOD, THE RECRUITING OFFICER, THE QUEEN AND I, KING LEAR (Max Stafford Clark), SORE THROATS (Nancy Duguid), SEARCH AND DESTROY (Stephen Daldry), ASHES AND SAND (Ian Rickson), OLEANNA (Harold Pinter), BERLIN BERTIE (Danny Boyle), OURSELVES ALONE, GREENLAND (Simon Curtis). Other theatre includes: THE FIFTEEN STREETS (Coventry/West End), PETER PAN (Leeds); TRUE WEST, FOOL FOR LOVE (Donmar); FENCES (Liverpool/West End); LYSISTRATA (Old Vic); BLUE REMEMBERED HILLS (Bristol); OF MICE AND MEN (Nottingham). Opera and musicals include: PORGY AND BESS (Trevor Nunn); OTELLO (Peter Stein); CARMEN (David Pountney); MARTIN GUERRE (Declan Donnellan); JESUS CHRIST SUPERSTAR (Gael Edwards); OLIVER (Sam Mendes); SATURDAY NIGHT FEVER (Arlene Philips); SPEND SPEND SPEND (Jeremy Sams); WEST SIDE STORY (West End); LAUTREC (Rob Bettinson). Work for television includes: THE BILL, CASUALTY, EASTENDERS, BROKEN GLASS, A KIND OF INNOCENCE, FELL TIGER, SCOLDS BRIDAL, FATAL INVERSION, NERYS GLAS, DEATH OF A SALESMAN, THE WIDOWING OF MRS HOLYROYD, MEASURE FOR MEASURE, THE MAYOR OF CASTERBRIDGE, LUCKY JIM, BLUE DOVE.

Billy McElhaney (Gary): Theatre Work includes: PASSING PLACES (Greenwich/Derby Playhouse); THE MEMORY OF WATER (Southampton Nuffield/Guildford); CALEDONIA DREAMING, REVOLTING PEASANTS (7:84); YOU'LL HAVE HAD YOUR HOLE (West Yorkshire Playhouse); ALADIN (His Majesty's); WE ARE THE HIBEES (Brunton/Gallus); TRUMPETS AND RASPBERRIES (Borderline); VIRTUAL REALITY (Montgomery Media); CITY LIGHTS TOUR (City Lights Touring); ANNUS HORRIBILUS (Wildcat); A MIDSUMMER NIGHTS DREAM, THE BEVELLERS, MACBETH (Royal Lyceum). Television work includes: THE YOUNG PERSON'S GUIDE TO BECOMING A ROCK STAR, THIS YEAR'S LOVE, LOOKING AFTER JOJO; THE ACID HOUSE; RAB C NESBITT, THE WINTER GUEST, THE BALDY MAN, ATHLETICO PARTICK, STAR, BAD BOYS, RUFFIAN HEARTS, PARAHANDY, TAGGART, BLOOD RED ROSES, SHOOT FOR THE SUN, A SHADOW ON EARTH, BROND. Film work includes: COMFORT AND JOY, HEAVENLY PURSUITS, SILENT SCREAM, ROB ROY.

Michael Moreland (Tom): Trained: RSAMD. Theatre Work includes: STROMA (TAG); PASSING PLACES (Greenwich/Derby Playhouse); JUNK (Oxford Stage Company/Manchester Library Theatre); THE COUNTRY WIFE (Bridewell); THE SEAL WIFE (Attic); WOOF! (Birmingham Stage); MACBETH (Chester Gateway). Television work includes: A TOUCH OF FROST, THE BILL, MAGIC WITH EVERYTHING, THIS LIFE. Film work includes: THE TRENCH, A TIME TO LOVE.

Michael Nardone (Eddie): Trained: Queen Margaret College, Edinburgh. For the Traverse: EUROPE, MARISOL, BUCHANAN, THE COLLECTION, WIDOWS, THE SPECULATOR (a co-production with the Edinburgh International Festival), KNIVES IN HENS (also at the Bush). Other Theatre: WILDMAN, SHINDA THE MAGIC APE, THE MARRIAGE OF FIGARO, MERLIN (parts 1 & 2) and MIRANDOLINA for the Royal Lyceum; SPLATTER for 7:84; BOUNCERS, CAIN AND ABEL for Chester Gateway; ELIDOR and TOM SAWYER for Contact Theatre, Manchester; THE LEGEND

OF ST JULIAN, TALES OF THE ARABIAN NIGHTS, CYRANO DE BERGERAC (also Almeida) for Communicado; WHAT EVERY WOMAN KNOWS for Newbury Theatre; ANE SATYRE OF THE FOURTH ESTAITE (WILDCAT/Edinburgh International Festival); THE CHEVIOT, THE STAG AND THE BLACK, BLACK OIL (Wildcat); VICTORIA (RSC); MEDEA (Theatre Babel). Television: DOCTOR FINLAY, TAGGART, RUTH RENDELL, CASUALTY, THE BILL, WYCLIFFE, LOOKING AFTER JOJO, TINSEL TOWN, THE CREATIVES, INSPECTOR REBUS. Film credits include: CONQUEST OF THE SOUTH POLE, SOFT TOP HARD SHOULDER, BEING HUMAN and THE MATCH.

Maurice Roëves (Frank): Trained: Glasgow Royal College of Music and Drama. Recent theatre includes: KILLING OF MICHAEL MALLOY (Los Angeles & Philadelphia, awarded LA Theater Award Best Actor 1994); TROUBLE IN MIND (Tricycle); THE BRAVE (Bush); OTHELLO, GOOD (Perth); TUNES OF GLORY (Citizens and Perth); THERE WAS A MAN (Edinburgh International Festival); MACBETH (Royal Court); ROMEO AND JULIET (Shaw). Television includes: GRAFTERS (Granada TV); THE SIGHT (Fox fx 2000); 919 FIFTH AVE (CBS TV); CHEERS (Paramount TV); BAYWATCH, STAR TREK - THE NEXT GENERATION (Fox TV); TUTTI FRUTTI (BBC)(Awarded Press Guild Award). Television films include: HILLSBOROUGH (Granada TV); DAVID, MOSES (TNT); THE NEGOTIATOR (BBC); INSIDE THE THIRD REICH (ABC TV). Recent films: BEAUTIFUL CREATURES (Universal Pictures 2000); ACID HOUSE TRILOGY (Umbrella Productions); LAST OF THE MOHICANS (20th Century Fox); JUDGE DREDD (Cinergi); HIDDEN AGENDA (Helmdale Pictures).

Mick Slaven (composer): Composed and played music for PASSING PLACES (Traverse Theatre Company and Tour). Plays guitar for the Leopards and records for Creeping Bent Records.

John Tiffany (director): Trained: Glasgow University. Literary Director at the Traverse since June 1997. For the Traverse: AMONG UNBROKEN HEARTS (also Bush), ABANDONMENT, KING OF THE FIELDS, THE JUJU GIRL, DANNY 306 + ME (4 EVER) (also Birmingham Rep), PERFECT DAYS (also Hampstead, Vaudeville and tour), GRETA, PASSING PLACES (also Citizens' and tour), SHARP SHORTS and STONES AND ASHES (co-director). Other theatre work includes: HIDE AND SEEK and BABY, EAT UP (LookOut); THE SUNSET SHIP (Young Vic); GRIMM TALES (Leicester Haymarket); EARTHQUAKE WEATHER (Starving Artists). Film includes: KARMIC MOTHERS (BBC Tartan Shorts) and GOLDEN WEDDING (BBC Two Lives).

Neil Warmington (designer): Graduated in Fine Art Painting at Maidstone College of Art before attending the post-graduate Theatre Design Course at Motley, London. For The Traverse: SOLEMN MASS FOR A FULL MOON IN SUMMER, KING OF THE FIELDS, FAMILY, PASSING PLACES (TMA Award for best design). Recent Theatre includes: SPLENDOUR, RIDDANCE - Fringe Firsts (Paines Plough); LOVES LABOURS LOST, DON JUAN, TAMING OF THE SHREW (English Touring Theatre); DESIRE UNDER THE ELMS, JANE EYRE - Barclays stage award for design (Shared Experience): THE DUCHESS OF MALFI (Bath Theatre Royal); WOYZECK, COMEDIANS, MERLIN, THE GLASS MENAGERIE (Royal Lyceum); DISSENT, ANGELS IN AMERICA (7:84); HENRY V (RSC), MUCH ADO ABOUT NOTHING (Queen's London), THE TEMPEST (Contact); WAITING FOR GODOT (Liverpool Everyman); FIDDLER ON THE ROOF, LIFE IS A DREAM -TMA award for Best Design (West Yorkshire Playhouse); TROILUS AND CRESSIDA (Opera North), OEDIPUS REX (Connecticut State Opera); MARRIAGE OF FIGARO (Garsington Opera). Designed the launch of Glasgow 1999 Year of Architecture. He has also won the Linbury prize for Stage Design and the Sir Alfred Munnings Florence prize for painting.

Chahine Yavroyan (lighting designer): Trained at the Bristol Old Vic Theatre School. For the Traverse: KING OF THE FIELDS, THE SPECULATOR, DANNY 306 + ME (4 EVER), PERFECT DAYS, KILL THE OLD TORTURE THEIR YOUNG, ANNA WEISS, KNIVES IN HENS, THE ARCHITECT and SHINING SOULS. He has worked extensively in theatre, with companies and artists including: Crucible, Royal Court, Nottingham Playhouse, Leicester Haymarket, ICA, ENO, Lindsay Kemp, Rose English, Pip Simmons. Dance work includes: Yolande Snaith Theatredance, Bock & Vincenzi, Anatomy Performance Company, Naheed Saddiqui. Chahine has also worked on many site specific works including Station House Opera, Dreamwork at St Pancras Chambers, Coin St Museum, City of Bologna, Italy New Year's Eve celebrations. Fashion shows for Givenchy, Chalayan, Clemens-Riberio, Ghost. He is also a long standing People Show Person.

**For generous help on GAGARIN WAY
the Traverse thanks:**

All the actors who workshopped the play: James Cunningham, Ron Donachie, Colin McCredie, Neil McKinven, Steven McNicoll, Neil James Ross, John Stahl

BLF

LEVER BROTHERS *for wardrobe care*

Sets, props and costumes for GAGARIN WAY created by Traverse Workshops
(funded by the National Lottery)

THE SCOTTISH ARTS COUNCIL
National Lottery Fund

production photography Kevin Low
print photography Euan Myles

SPONSORSHIP

Sponsorship income enables the Traverse to commission and produce new plays and to offer audiences a diverse and exciting programme of events throughout the year.

We would like to thank the following companies for their support throughout the year:

CORPORATE ASSOCIATE SCHEME

MAJOR SPONSORS

Sunday Herald
Scottish Life the PENSION company
United Distillers & Vintners
Laurence Smith & Son Wine Merchants
Willis Corroon Scotland Ltd
Wired Nomad
Alistir Tait FGA - Antiques & Fine Jewellery
Nicholas Groves Raines - Architects
KPMG
The Post Office
Amanda Howard Associates
Alan Thienot Champagne
Bairds Fine and Country Wines

The Traverse Trivia Quiz in association with Tennents

With thanks to: Navy Blue Design Consultants & Stewarts, graphic designers and printers for the Traverse
Arts & Business for management and mentoring services
Purchase of the Traverse Box Office, computer network and technical and training equipment has been made possible with money from The Scottish Arts Council National Lottery Fund

The Traverse Theatre's work would not be possible without the support of

THE CITY OF EDINBURGH COUNCIL

The Traverse receives financial assistance for its educational and development work from
Calouste Gulbenkian Foundation, John Lewis Partnership, Peggy Ramsay Foundation, The Yapp Charitable Trusts, Binks Trust, The Bulldog Prinsep Theatrical Trust, Esmee Fairbairn Trust, Gannochy Trust, Gordon Fraser Charitable Trust, The Garfield Weston Foundation, JSP Pollitzer Charitable Trust, The Hope Trust, The Steel Trust, Paul Hamlyn Foundation, The Craignish Trust, Lindsay's Charitable Trust, Tay Charitable Trust.

Charity No. SC002368

TRAVERSE THEATRE - THE COMPANY

Gregory Burke
Gagarin Way

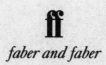

faber and faber

First published in 2001
by Faber and Faber Limited
3 Queen Square, London WC1N 3AU
Published in the United States by Faber and Faber Inc.
an affiliate of Farrar, Straus and Giroux LLC, New York

Typeset by Country Setting, Kingsdown, Kent CT14 8ES
Printed in England by Mackays of Chatham plc, Chatham, Kent

A CIP record for this book
is available from the British Library

ISBN 0–571–21236–0

2 4 6 8 10 9 7 5 3

Characters

Tom
a security guard, early twenties

Eddie
a factory worker, early thirties

Gary
a factory worker, late thirties, powerfully built

Frank
fifties, tall, grey hair

*The scene takes place at night in a storeroom which is
part of a factory. There is a door with a small window,* empty
and piles of boxes lining the walls. Several boxes, to be stage
*used as seats, are on the floor. Two men are on stage.
Tom, wearing a security guard's uniform, is standing
with his back to the wall near the door. Eddie, wearing
a Stone Island jacket, jeans and trainers, is looking
through the window in the door.*

Eddie It's no fucking him.

Tom (*whispers*) No?

Eddie No.

   Pause.

Tom (*whispers*) Who was it?

Eddie I dinnay ken . . . just some cunt turning ay. (*Turns
away from the window.*) What are you whispering for?

Tom (*whispers*) I don't know.

Eddie Stop it.

Tom Sorry. (*Beat.*) I'm just . . . nervous.

Eddie No need for nerves. (*Pause.*) It was a bit quick tay
be Gary ay.

   Pause.

Tom (*moves nervously into the centre of the room and
sits down*) So what was it you were saying about Sartre?

Eddie I wasnay saying anything about him. It was you
that was talking about him.

Tom You said he was shite.

Eddie I never said he was shite.

Tom You did.

Eddie I never. (*Beat.*) I said I'll give the cunt his due. He came up with some snappy titles for his books. *Being and Nothingness* is a good fucking title for a book ken. But he had tay give them snappy titles tay get them shifted before folk discovered the shite that was inside.

Tom It's a critique of sorts I suppose.

Eddie I've never understood why the cunt gets so much credit ay. Sitting around in a café all day way they big fucking bug eyes. I mean if he's so fucking clever how come he got the pish taken out ay him by Jean Genet?

Tom Who?

Eddie Jean Genet.

Tom Who was he?

Eddie He was a thief.

Tom A thief?

Eddie Aye, and no just like a wee bit ay a rascal ken . . . more your dyed-in-the-wool, incorrigible cutpurse. Couldnay keep his hands off what wasnay his.

Tom Nice.

Eddie He'd a wee bit ay a literary sideline going tay ken. I mean, even then every criminal worth his salt had tay have a literary sideline going ay. He bashed out a load ay stuff about going round Europe thieving and hawking his arse. Sartre thought it was magic and like adopted him . . . ken as like a wee novelty act for taking tay parties and that, ken like as the cabaret. Bit ay juggling. Bit ay underclass anecdote. Star ay the fucking show.

Couldnay get enough ay him in the salons. (*Beat*.) You
ken yourself ay . . . there's nothing the general public
likes better than a <u>vicarious wander through the world</u>
<u>ay the full-time criminal</u>. And if you've got yourself the
tear-jerking childhood tay back it up . . . make a fucking
mint.

we are experiencing a 'wander'

    Pause.

Tom And did he? Make a mint?

Eddie Well . . . see . . . he couldnay . . . I dinnay think
the money fay the scribbling, or anything else like, was
ever gonnay be enough tay overcome his natural
tendencies.

Tom <u>It's a precarious profession</u>. Writing.

Eddie You've got tay have something tay fall back on.
Robbing was what he knew best. Only drawback was he
had an awfy tendency tay get collared . . . they had this
thing in France . . . I cannay mind its name . . . like what
they have in America . . . ken, if you keep getting caught
for the same thing you get life.

Tom Three strikes and you're out.

Eddie Aye . . . the French had like one word for it . . . *la*
something . . . or *le* something . . . I cannay mind, anyway
he keeps getting caught and he ends up way a life sentence
for having the stickiest fucking mitts in France.

Tom Quite right too.

Eddie That's no the best bit. I mean your average
civilian might say good fucking riddance. Horse the cunt
tay Devil's Island and chuck away the key. But no the
fucking intelligentsia ay. Oh no, soon as they find out
Genet's got a one-way ticket, all the café-dwellers are up
at the prison gates demanding he gets let out. (*Beat*.)
And why?

7

Tom I don't know.

Eddie Jean-Paul Sartre's come up way one ay his theories and it turns out Genet's no really a thief after all.

Tom No?

Eddie (*moves into the centre of the room*) It's nothing tay day way kleptomania. (*Beat.*) Oh no, all Genet's doing is authenticating himself in existentialist terms by choosing tay be the thief that every cunt's been saying he was since he started nicking things when he was a bairn. (*Beat.*) Have you ever heard the fucking like? Please your honour the philosophers made me day it. (*Beat.*) See if you tried a defence like that here . . .

Tom Laughed out of court.

Eddie They'd give you an extra couple ay years for wasting their time. (*Beat.*) But it's France . . . the more outlandish the intellectual pish . . . the quicker they fall for it.

Tom They let him off?

Eddie Couldnay return him tay society quick enough.

Tom Amazing.

Eddie And way his new, cast-iron, Jean-Paul Sartre provided excuse tay go wherever the fuck his light fingers take him. (*Beat.*) First stop Sartre's gaff tay have it on his toes way the family silver.

Tom Proves the theory.

Eddie (*moves to stand over Tom*) I mean the cunt might be the number one living example ay the point you're trying tay make, but the last thing you need after a hard day's gibbering pish on the left bank about how we're all subjects among objects, is finding out you're a subject among no as many objects now you've got fucking Jean Genet out ay the jail.

Tom Hell is other people.

Eddie Especially when they flog your telly for ten francs and a feel at an Arab's arse. (*Beat.*) Any cunt who comes up way a theory that thieves are only interested in your gear so they can achieve coincidence ay the consciousness ay the subject way it's own objective reality is a fanny. (*Pause.*) What was it you said you did at university?

   Pause.

Tom Politics.

Eddie Politics.

Tom And economics. (*Beat.*) And a little bit of philosophy. (*Beat.*) A tiny little bit.

Eddie A tiny little bit.

Tom In first year. (*Beat.*) I don't remember much about it.

Eddie You can mind being there, but nothing about it.

Tom Four years ago now, first year.

Eddie A lifetime. (*Pause.*) So what made you want tay try out your tiny little bit ay philosophical knowledge on me?

Tom It was just . . . conversation.

Eddie Trying tay blind a dumb fuck way the dazzling breadth ay your learning.

Tom No. (*Pause.*) You seem to know a lot about it?

Eddie Conversation?

Tom Philosophy.

Eddie It's amazing what you can day way a library ticket.

Pause.

Tom (*stands up, moves back to the door and looks out of the window*) How much longer do you think?

Eddie (*sits down*) Soon.

Tom What time did he say he'd be here?

Eddie He didnay say . . . like exactly ken. (*Beat.*) Plenty fucking time.

Pause.

Tom You should have arranged an exact time.

Eddie If you want tay keep an eye out go back down tay your howf. You'll hay tay open the gate for him anyway.

Tom (*turns to face Eddie*) It's just as difficult to see up the road from there . . . the way it bends. (*Moves back into the middle of the room.*) I'll wait.

Pause.

Eddie (*indicates a box*) Sit down then ay.

Tom (*remains standing. Removes his hat and puts it down on the box. Wipes his face with his sleeve*) It's boiling in here.

Eddie It's always warm in here. (*Pause.*) It's been a pish summer though ay.

Tom Whatever happened to global warming?

Eddie Aye. It's a shame about that ay.

Tom A shame?

Eddie Aye. (*Beat.*) You ken we're no getting global warming ay?

Tom No.

Eddie It's gonnay be global apart fay us.

Tom Aye?

Eddie Something tay day way the Gulf Stream. The world heats up . . . the polar cap recedes . . . we stop getting the Gulf Stream . . . the world gets warmer, we get colder.

Tom You're joking.

Eddie Straight up. (*Beat.*) A boy in the pub told me.

Tom Ironic.

Eddie Typical. I mean they coulday at least . . . like in among all the scare stories and that . . . put in brackets ken . . . 'apart fay Scotland'. Stop us getting our fucking hopes up ay. (*Beat.*) Gonnay sit down.

Tom I'm fine.

Eddie Sit down.

Tom I'm fine.

Eddie I'd rather you sat down.

Tom I can keep an eye on the door.

Eddie It'll be a wee while yet.

Tom I don't mind.

Eddie I want you to sit down. (*Beat.*) So fucking sit down.

Tom (*sits down*) How many times have you done this?

Eddie Sat in a factory talking pish tay some cunt I hardly ken.

Tom Aye.

Eddie Loads.

Tom And stealing computer chips.

Eddie Loads.

Tom Never had any trouble.

Eddie Never. There's always plenty boys like yourself needing tay top up their wages ay. (*Beat.*) I'll maybe keep you in mind for the next time.

Tom Next time?

Eddie A couple ay months maybe.

Tom I won't be here long enough for that.

Eddie No?

Tom No.

Eddie They all say that.

Tom I'm waiting to hear about a job.

Eddie Is it shagging supermodels for eighty pound an hour? (*Beat.*) That's the sort ay job I see you in ken. Security . . . it's just so below you.

   Pause.

Tom I'm in for five at the moment. (*Beat.*) Jobs. (*Beat.*) I'm bound to get one of them. (*Beat.*) Even though I got a two-two. (*Beat.*) Which was a bit disappointing.

Eddie You can day anything.

Tom But not a complete disaster.

Eddie Flip burgers.

Tom It could've been worse.

Eddie Stack shelves.

Tom Someone'll want me.

Eddie Arenay worth the paper they're written on . . . degrees . . . all these new unis and that . . . this place'll be full ay graduates in a few years.

   Pause.

Tom I've done enough shite jobs to get by. This isn't even the worst. At least I don't have to deal with the public.

Eddie I couldnay deal way the public. (*Beat.*) Which kinday limits me in a service-driven economy.

Tom It's torture. You've no idea how mental people are. I worked in this call centre. Now that's real slavery. Hooked up to a machine all day. Taped all the time. Timed all the time. They even time you going to the bog.

Eddie It'll be catheters next.

Tom And all the time stupid, mental members of the public moaning at you. (*Beat.*) At least this gives me time to myself.

Eddie So what are you bothering me for?

Tom I was bored.

   Pause.

Eddie (*stands up and moves to sit beside Tom*) There was this cunt worked in here up until a couple ay years ago ay. I kent him fay school like. He was like the total high-flier ay the school ken. Destined for the fucking top. (*Beat.*) I dinnay ken whether he dropped out ay uni or what happened ay, but it had all gone pear-shaped for the cunt somewhere along the line. (*Beat.*) He thought he was a right fucking smartarse. Really arrogant ken.

Far too good tay be mixing way the likes ay us. (*Beat*.)
A couple ay cunts even had tay bang him he was that
fucking wide. (*Beat*.) He used tay get the pish ripped out
ay him like. Non-fucking-stop. Most cunts would ay
laughed it off ay, but he used tay get really wound up.
And I mean like really wound up ken. (*Beat*.) I didnay
think he woulday jumped off the bridge mind.

Tom Did he die?

Eddie Aye well it does tend tay happen when you jump
off something that high ken. (*Beat*.) It was probably for
the best. You dinnay ken what sort ay sick, serial-killer
road he might ay ended up wandering down ay. (*Beat*.)
I'd hate tay see that happen tay you.

Tom It won't.

Eddie Aye, but maybe you won't get the job you want
ay. You'll have tay keep doing this for a bit longer.
Maybe after about a year you'll start getting a wee bit
frustrated.

Tom I bet you any amount of money you like I won't
be here a year from now.

Eddie You'll be up the toon quietly sipping at a pint.
(*Mimes drinking*.) Some cunt you used tay know at
school spots you.

Tom I won't even be here in a month.

Eddie They'll be like . . . so what are you up tay now . . .
you tell them and they'll be like . . . ya cunt, I thought
you were a clever bastard . . . and you'll be like, oh aye,
ha, ha, big joke and that, security guard, ha, ha, big
fucking joke. (*Beat*.) And then the depression starts . . .
nagging at the back ay your self-esteem. You'll start
feeling a wee bit bitter.

Tom I don't think so.

Eddie It drags on a wee bit longer.

Tom It won't happen.

Eddie Another year in here.

Tom No chance.

Eddie You start feeling cheated.

Tom Piss off.

Eddie Thinking there's a bit ay a conspiracy out there . . . against you.

Tom Fuck off.

Eddie You start being like a wee bit reclusive. Shit feared ay going out and meeting anyone in case you have tay explain. All your mates and that, they're like going fucking places . . . forging careers in the professions . . . aspiring all over the shop . . . leaving you behind. (*Beat.*) There's always one cunt, statistically like, that doesnay get the breaks.

Tom Was it you that made him jump?

Eddie The only solution is the bridge.

Pause.

Tom I could never kill myself.

Eddie No?

Tom No.

Pause.

Eddie A fantastic option, suicide. (*Beat.*) We're lucky tay have it.

Pause.

Tom If I was going to do it, I think pills would be best.

Eddie Better than the base jump or ritual disembowelment?

Tom No pain.

Eddie A good cowardly way out.

Tom I couldn't shoot myself.

Eddie No?

Tom A big bottle of paracetemol.

Eddie Tricky things tay manage . . . pill suicides. You've got tay decide whether you want tay make it your bog standard, survivable, cry for help or a serious death attempt. The last thing you need is tay go for an attention-seeker, go a wee bit too far but no far enough and end up hooked up tay a dialysis machine for the rest of your days.

Tom Nightmare.

Eddie Fucking laughing stock.

   Pause.

Tom (*stands up, crosses the room, and sits down.*) How long have you worked here?

   Pause.

Eddie Seven year.

Tom Seven years?

Eddie Aye.

Tom How have you managed it?

Eddie I guess I'm just lucky.

Tom I can't imagine working anywhere for seven years.

Eddie I suppose there must be something lacking in my character or something ay. (*Beat.*) I can mind my first day . . . thinking, after about ten minutes, fuck this

16

fucking shite, soon as I get a tea break I'm off. (*Beat.*)
I stuck it tay lunchtime, got chatting tay a couple ay
cunts in the canteen. (*Beat.*) Seven fucking years.

Pause.

Tom So how haven't you jumped off the bridge yet?

Eddie Well I wouldnay rule it out. (*Beat.*) There's still
one or two things I've got tay try first.

Tom What things?

Eddie Just . . . ken . . . ideas.

Pause.

Tom How old are you?

Eddie Thirty-two.

Tom Really.

Eddie Fucking thirty-two.

Tom You don't look it.

Eddie I dinnay fucking feel it. (*Beat.*) Well . . . I day
sometimes ken. (*Beat.*) I've got my middle youth at least.

Pause.

Tom Are you married?

Eddie No. (*Beat.*) I used tay live way a lassie like. (*Beat.*)
Well . . . I say lived way her . . . more ponced off her
really ay. (*Beat.*) It's tough when your salaries arenay
compatible. (*Beat.*) I didnay object tay her being the
main breadwinner like . . . she was the old-fashioned
one. I thought she woulday, ken . . . fucking applauded
my willingness tay abdicate fay the traditional male
role . . . but she couldnay understand why I didnay
want equality. (*Beat.*) I mean I'm no a bad-looking cunt.
I coulday been a fucking trophy husband ay?

Tom Eh . . . aye.

Eddie Cooking . . . cleaning . . . aerobics . . . facials . . .
I'd ay been quite fucking happy.

Tom It's a terrible thing, sexism.

Eddie It's a cunt.

> *Eddie gets up and crosses the room to look through
> the window in the door. Tom stands up. Eddie turns
> away from the door shaking his head.*

Tom (*sits down*) They always sound louder at night.
The cars. I think they're coming down the road when
they're over on the dual carriageway too. (*Beat.*) I didn't
realise there was a black market in computer chips.

Eddie There's a black market in everything.

Tom Who buys them?

Eddie You dinnay expect me tay tell you? (*Beat.*) I dinnay
really ken myself ay. It's Gary's brother. He's got the
contacts. We just pass them on.

Tom Bit of a lad is he?

Eddie Gary's brother?

Tom Aye.

Eddie (*leaves the door*) Very naughty. (*Sits down beside
Tom.*) Drugs. Guns. Catamites. He's your man. (*Beat.*)
Day you go up the toon?

Tom I used to.

Eddie You'll maybe ken him. He's a bouncer. Works all
over. Gets called Bananas.

Tom Mental is he?

Eddie No, he owns a fucking fruit shop.

> *Pause.*

Tom I've not been up the town for ages.

Eddie You're no missing anything. The alpha males are still out in force. The gene pool's still as shallow. (*Beat.*) It's no the same though . . . no sailors tay fight since they shut the yard . . . fucking peace dividend . . . cameras everywhere . . . it's pish.

Tom He won't let you down?

Eddie Gary? (*Beat.*) No chance. He's a top bloke. An *über-untermensch* if ever there was one. (*Beat.*) Unhappy like. But who fucking isnay?

Tom Unhappy?

Eddie Ken . . . pupped his bird on the first shag and before he kent he hated her he had three bairns, a dog and a depression. (*Beat.*) He'd never let his mates down.

 Pause.

Tom Hard is he? (*Beat.*) Like his brother?

Eddie Hard as fuck. (*Beat.*) Right on the verge ay collapse.

 Pause.

Tom He should get help.

Eddie It's no an easy thing tay admit tay . . . ken . . . even now . . . some cunts ay . . . the stigma's still a bit too much tay handle.

 Pause.

Tom He should get signed off.

Eddie There's no sick pay.

 Pause.

Tom He should do a runner.

Eddie I think he's maybe got attached tay the bairns . . . ken . . . like through time and that . . . what day you call it?

Tom What?

Eddie Osmosis. That's what you call it ay? Osmosis.

Tom Osmosis.

Eddie If a bairn's there . . . hanging round all the time . . . you cannay help but get attached.

Tom moves to the window.

Tom How long has he worked here?

Eddie About four or five year. (*Beat.*) He was in the dockyard before that. He was a shop steward down there and all like. Quite a . . . ken . . . a firebrand.

Tom One of the old school.

Eddie First in the queue for redundancy. (*Beat.*) Spent it all. Had tay get three jobs.

Pause.

Tom My old boy worked in the yard.

Eddie Aye.

Tom (*moves back to the centre of the room*) He was an accountant . . . in the end like. He was a shipwright to trade . . . in there all his days . . . ended up as an accountant. He took his early retirement too. He's got a post office now.

Eddie What're the alarms like?

Tom He was only fifty-two . . . too young to retire.

Eddie That's fuck all. I had a mate took early retirement when he was twenty-four.

Tom Twenty-four.

Eddie It wasnay really early retirement ay . . . it was redundancy . . . but we used tay kid him on about being retired ken. He done it tay get the money tay go round the world. (*Beat.*) He only got as far as Amsterdam.

Tom Amsterdam. (*Beat.*) Understandable.

Eddie He had loads ay money ay. He coulday gone round the world about four fucking times. Amsterdam was his first stop.

Tom I went with the uni . . . eh hockey team . . . for a tournament. We never even got round tay playing any games.

Eddie All that money in his pocket. It's fucking five-star hotels, hookers and more charlie than you can shake a hockey stick at. (*Beat.*) He ended up setting his head on fire . . . accidentally like. He had this massive line ay charlie along the table in his hotel room but he'd like put these candles . . . on the table ken. He's snorting the line . . . hair goes in the candle. (*Beat.*) Nasty business.

Tom Hurt bad?

Eddie He was alright. (*Beat.*) He just had tay suffer the humiliation ay coming back tay the toon after three weeks, skint, way a big fucking burn on the top ay his head.

   Pause.

Tom I'd love to do something like that.

Eddie I'll go and look for a candle.

Tom Go round the world. (*Beat.*) I might do it after I've paid off all my debts.

Eddie Never, then.

   Pause.

Tom I was in Israel a couple of summers ago . . . On a kibbutz. It was near this place, Masada, where like all these zealots . . . Jews like . . . killed themselves rather than surrender to the Romans. (*Beat.*) I didn't stay long.

Eddie Too many hippies on them kibbutz things ay.

Tom It wasn't that. I just didn't like the place. Israel like . . . I mean it's beautiful . . . but scary. It was peace then, supposed to be. Peace. (*Beat.*) Everybody had guns. Everybody. They were all just waiting for the next war. Sitting . . . armed to the teeth . . . waiting.

Eddie Aye well nay wonder ay. You cannay blame the cunts for having a bit ay a chip on their shoulder. (*Beat.*) I think, ken that there's like certain privileged people when it comes tay . . . ken . . . keeping themselves occupied and that ay . . . having something tay day. Israelis and Palestinians and that . . . ken . . . they've got something tay aim for.

Tom Each other.

Eddie Aye . . . each fucking other. (*Beat.*) It's bollocks though ay . . . travel. (*Beat.*) I mean I can maybe understand that like . . . ken that sort ay menopause that hits every cunt about the mid-twenties mark . . . when they think the job and the bird doesnay provide the answers, so they chuck it in and they fuck off. I can understand that . . . 'cause a month later they're back when they realise, after all, ken, they day actually prefer Stone Island jackets, good music and a bird that shaves under her arms. (*Beat.*) It's these fucking cunts that think if they spend a summer on an island somewhere, fucking some goat-counter, that they're on their way tay a unifying theory ay the universe, ken, or fucking off up some hill tay purify their fucking spirit. (*Beat.*) There's fuck all at the tops ay mountains bar thinner fucking air.

The noise of a van engine.

Tom (*moves over to look out of the window*) Is that him?

Eddie (*joins him*) You better go and open the gate.

Tom Right.

Eddie We'll no be long.

   Pause.

Tom What about?

Eddie Later in the week.

Tom Right.

Eddie Give it a few days just tay be on the safe side. I'll sort you out then.

Tom Right.

   Pause.

Eddie Go on then, fuck off.

Tom See you. (*Exits.*)

Eddie Wanker. (*Gets a box and places it in the centre of the room. Fidgets about nervously.*)

   A van draws up outside. Gary enters. He is wearing a long black coat and is carrying Frank in a fireman's lift. Frank is tied, hooded and unconscious. Gary lowers Frank onto the box in the centre of the room.

Alright?

Gary (*closes the door*) Aye.

   Pause.

Eddie Everything . . . alright?

Gary Aye . . . nay bother.

Gary I dinnay ken what that cunt was up tay. (*Indicates outside.*) He wasnay in his howf.

Eddie He was in here.

Gary In here?

Eddie Aye.

Gary What was he wanting in here?

Eddie Just hanging about. Gibbering pish.

Gary Aye . . . but.

Eddie Dinnay worry.

Gary You didnay say . . .

Eddie Dinnay be daft. (*Beat.*) He's no got a fucking clue.

Gary You sure.

Eddie Aye. (*Beat.*) Everything go alright aye?

Gary Aye. (*Beat.*) Well . . . one thing ay.

Eddie You took your time.

Gary You cannay rush something like this.

Eddie Aye.

Gary I had tay wait for my moment.

 Eddie stands staring at Gary.

What?

Eddie What's that?

Gary What?

Eddie (*points at Gary's coat*) That?

Gary What? (*Beat.*) It's a coat. (*Beat.*) What?

Eddie Nothing.

24

Gary What's wrong way it?

Eddie Nothing. (*Pause.*) Did you get the . . .

Gary (*reaches inside his coat and pulls out a large McDonald's paper bag which he hands to Eddie*) There you go.

Eddie (*opens the bag and looks inside*) Lovely.

Gary Did you get the balaclavas?

Eddie (*puts the bag down on top of a box. Looks down at Frank*) Is he alright?

Gary Aye. (*Beat.*) Did you get the . . .

Eddie He doesnay look alright.

Gary He's fine.

Eddie What the fuck did you hit him way?

Gary (*pulls out a cosh*) This. (*Beat.*) Did you get the balaclavas?

   Pause.

Eddie No.

Gary No?

Eddie We dinnay need them.

Gary Aye, we day.

Eddie How?

Gary (*indicates Frank*) He'll see our faces.

Eddie Doesnay matter.

Gary Aye it does.

Eddie How?

Gary How? (*Beat.*) He can identify us, that's how.

Eddie Doesnay matter.

Gary I dinnay fucking believe this. (*Beat.*) It was part ay the plan.

    Pause.

Eddie You've no changed your mind?

    Pause.

Gary No.

Eddie No need for fucking balaclavas then ay?

    Pause.

Gary No.

    Pause.

Eddie (*looks at Frank*) Are you sure he's okay?

Gary Aye.

    Pause.

Eddie He's taller than you'd think ay.

Gary Aye.

Eddie I thought he'd be wee'er.

Gary Aye.

Eddie Must be putting something in the noodles.

Gary Listen. (*Beat.*) That's what I was gonnay tell you.

Eddie What?

Gary He's no fucking Japanese.

    Pause.

Eddie He's no Japanese?

Gary No.

Pause.

Eddie So what the fuck is he then?

Gary I day ken. (*Beat.*) He's like us.

Eddie Like us?

Gary Aye . . . like . . . ken . . . like us.

Eddie Us?

Gary You and me . . . us.

Pause.

Eddie European?

Gary Aye. Eurofuckinpean.

Eddie You're fucking joking?

Gary No.

Eddie You are joking ay?

Gary Take a look.

Eddie (*pulls the hood from Frank's head to reveal a silver-haired European male*) Bastard.

Gary I was in the right room.

Eddie I cannay believe this.

Gary It was kinday dark mind.

Eddie Every time they've sent someone here they've been a fucking Chinky.

Gary When I got him.

Eddie Every fucking time.

Gary Way rushing and that . . . I didnay really notice.

Eddie Till now.

Gary When I seen he wasnay . . . (*Pause. Pulls a security pass from his pocket and gives it to Eddie.*)

Eddie (*looks at the card*) F. Van de Hoy. (*Beat.*) Van de Hoy. Must be Dutch. Somewhere round about there anyway.

Gary Aye. (*Beat.*) I wonder what the F's for?

Eddie Who gives a fuck what the fucking F's for.

Pause.

Gary What day you think?

Pause.

Eddie (*hands the card back to Gary. Pause*) He works for this lot.

Gary Aye I ken but . . .

Eddie He's well up the pecking order.

Gary But he's no . . .

Eddie He's what we wanted.

Gary It's no the fucking same as a chinky . . . a Jap though.

Eddie He'll fucking day.

Gary The whole point was tay get a Jap.

Eddie It doesnay matter where he's fucking from.

Gary Aye it does.

Eddie Well what are you gonnay day? (*Beat.*) Take the cunt back tay the fucking hotel?

Gary No.

Eddie This cunt . . . he was gonnay come in here tomorrow and walk about . . . looking at us. You ken how you feel when they day that.

Gary I fucking hate it.

Eddie Walking about . . . looking at us . . . deciding our fate.

Gary Cunt.

Pause.

Eddie He's maybe American.

Gary That would be alright.

Eddie Aye.

Gary That would be braw. (*Pause.*) No very fat though. (*Beat.*) If he was gonnay be American.

Pause.

Eddie He's maybe Californian. (*Beat.*) A healthy cunt. (*Beat.*) Runs. Swims. Eats the tofu. (*Pause.*) What sort ay names day Americans call themselves?

Gary I day ken. (*Beat.*) Same as us ay.

Pause.

Eddie Chip.

Pause.

Gary He doesnay look like a Chip.

Tom enters.

Tom Sorry boys. I forgot my hat. (*Moves to get his hat from on top of a box. Stops when he sees Frank lying on the floor.*) Who's this? (*Pause. To Eddie.*) What's going on? (*Pause. To Gary.*) Who's this?

Gary pulls out his cosh and hits Tom with it. Tom falls.

Eddie (*looks down at Tom. To Gary*) He's definitely fucking dead.

Gary I hardly touched him.

Pause.

Eddie Mind you, he deserves it . . . prick.

Gary What's he like?

Eddie He's a prick. (*Beat.*) Bit ay a student.

Gary Aye?

Eddie Oh aye. Straight outay uni.

Gary What's he doing working as a security guard?

Eddie This is just a temporary thing before he launches himself into the employment stratosphere.

Gary An achiever.

Eddie I doubt it . . . no the brightest ay. Didnay study the right sort ay subject tay achieve anything. (*Beat.*) He did politics.

Gary Did he?

Eddie Aye. (*Pause. Looks at Gary.*) Mind you?

Gary What?

Eddie It doesnay matter.

Gary What?

Eddie Nothing.

Pause.

Gary What?

Eddie You'll no like it.

Gary What?

Eddie I was thinking . . . we could ask him . . . tay join in.

Gary Steady.

Eddie No like join in join in . . .

Gary He cannay just join in.

Eddie He'd be perfect.

Gary How?

Eddie He's got a degree. (*Beat.*) In politics.

Gary It's just you and me.

Eddie Aye, but if this . . . ken . . . what we're daying . . . we're gonnay have tay judge public reaction ay . . . and cunts like this (*indicates Tom*) are the folk it's probably gonnay appeal tay. (*Beat.*) He's a worker.

Gary You said he was a student.

Eddie He's a civilian.

Pause.

Gary He could be like . . . a focus group.

Eddie Exactly.

Pause.

Gary Only one way tay find out.

Eddie and Gary begin shaking and slapping Tom.

Eddie Wake up, cunt.

Tom begins to move.

Gary See . . . just a tap.

Eddie (*to Gary*) Thick-skulled.

Gary (*to Tom*) Can you get up? (*Gary lifts Tom up and sits him on a box.*)

Gary (*to Tom*) You okay?

Tom What's . . .

Gary (*to Tom*) A misunderstanding.

Tom My head . . .

Gary Sorry. (*Beat.*) I didnay want tay hurt you.

Eddie I didnay want him tay hurt you.

Gary You're just a worker like us.

Eddie We dinnay want tay hurt folk like us.

Tom (*to Eddie*) I thought . . . you were stealing.

Eddie I'm afraid I've no been . . . straight way you.

    Pause.

Tom (*to Eddie, indicating Gary*) Is it to do with his brother?

Gary Eh?

Tom Is it . . . gangster stuff?

Gary (*to Tom*) Day you ken my brother? (*to Eddie*) Does he ken my brother?

Tom (*to Gary*) He told me.

Gary Oh aye. (*to Eddie*) What else have you been telling him?

Tom (*to Gary*) Is it a contract?

Gary Contract?

Tom Like a hit.

Eddie A hit? (*Beat.*) No. (*Hits Tom.*) That's a fucking hit.

Gary (*to Tom*) Listen. It's nothing tay day way my brother. This (*indicating Frank*) is Mister F. Van de Hoy. (*Beat.*) We dinnay ken what the F's for.

Eddie He's a visiting member ay senior management.

Gary One ay the top brass.

Tom He's coming tomorrow.

Gary He's here now.

Eddie We kidnapped him.

Tom Kidnapped?

Eddie It's a technical term.

Pause.

Tom What are you going to do with him?

Eddie We wait for him to come round. We have a chat about our objections tay multinational capitalism, (*picks up the paper bag and pulls out a gun*) then we shoot the cunt.

Pause. Tom begins to hyperventilate.

Gary This is all we fucking need.

Tom falls onto his knees.

Eddie It's a complication.

Tom falls flat on his face.

Gary A complication? It's a fucking disaster. (*Pause.*) What's he daying?

Eddie Dying, hopefully.

Gary Is he having a fit?

Eddie I'm no doctor like . . . but my diagnosis is he's hyperventilating.

Pause.

33

Gary It's a fucking noisy way tay go ay.

Eddie Aye.

Pause.

Gary Better day something.

Eddie Aye.

Gary Cannay just stand and watch.

Pause.

Eddie You need a bag. (*Kicks the paper bag the gun was in to Gary.*)

Gary (*places the bag over Tom's mouth*) Come on now . . . breathe. Nice and easy.

Tom's breathing begins to return to normal.

That's it. (*helping Tom up*) Sit up.

Tom sits up on a box.

You shouldnay have come back for your hat.

Eddie (*to Tom*) That's the trouble way hats. (*Picks up the hat.*) Spurious symbol ay authority . . . and liable tay drag you intay all sorts ay shit no ay your own making.

Gary You shoulday waited till we left.

Tom I didn't want to lose it. (*Beat.*) You have to pay for a new one.

Eddie places the hat on Tom's head.

(*to Eddie*) Can I go now?

Eddie I'm afraid not.

Gary You're going naywhere.

Tom begins to hyperventilate again.

34

Eddie (*pushes Tom's face back into the bag*) Get your head back in there and stop worrying. (*Moves to look at Frank.*) He's alright ay?

Gary He's alright.

Tom (*joins them*) He doesn't look too good.

Gary What?

Tom (*removes the bag from his face*) He doesn't look too good.

Eddie That's what I thought.

Gary He's alright.

Eddie How do you know?

Gary I'm fucking telling you he's alright. Alright. (*Stands up.*) Just give him a wee bit ay time.

   Pause.

Tom I don't want anything to do with this.

Eddie (*to Tom*) Too late.

Tom I could just go. I wouldn't say anything to anyone. (*Heads for the door.*) You can trust me.

Eddie (*follows Tom*) No . . . Tom . . . stay . . . Tom. (*Puts his arm round Tom, guiding him back to the centre of the room and forcing him to sit.*) We need tay talk about this.

Tom There's nothing to talk about.

Eddie There's loads tay talk about.

Gary (*to Tom*) Where are you gonnay go anyway? Your fucking wee sentry box doon at the gate where you sit and sleep at night?

Eddie You gonnay go home and pull the foreskin over your head?

Gary You gonnay go to the polis?

Eddie You have tay stay.

Pause.

Tom You said all I had to do was open the gate for you.

Gary That was all you had tay day.

Eddie You thought . . . two hundred quid for opening a door . . . that's alright.

Gary What were you daying hinging about anyway?

Eddie Easy money.

Gary You shoulday fucked off soon as you let him in.

Tom We just got talking.

Gary Well you've talked your way intay this.

Tom runs for the door. Gary chases him and wrestles him to the floor, puts him in an arm lock and drags him back into the middle of the room.

Tom You're breaking my arm.

Gary I'll break your fucking neck, you little cunt. (*to Eddie*) Get something tay tie him up way.

Eddie What?

Gary I day ken . . . fucking rope.

Eddie Where fay?

Tom (*to Gary*) It's gonnay break.

Tom screams.

Gary (*to Eddie. Indicates Frank*) You'll hay tay untie that cunt.

Eddie What if he wakes up?

Gary Too fucking bad.

Eddie unties Frank and brings the rope to Gary. They tie Tom's hands and lift him to his feet.

Tom (*shouts*) Help.

Gary Shut up.

Eddie Let him. (*to Tom*) Nay cunt can hear you.

Gary and Eddie drag Tom back to the centre of the room and force him to sit down.

(*to Tom*) I day ken what your problem is.

Gary Calm fucking down.

Eddie It's nothing tay day way you.

Gary You're worried about something that's nothing tay day way you.

Eddie You're charging about here . . . panicking . . . making every cunt nervous.

Gary Making me hurt you.

Eddie We don't want tay hurt you.

Gary No.

Eddie We're your friends.

Pause.

Gary (*to Tom*) If you knew why we were killing him you might no be so . . . opposed.

Eddie Listen tay the man.

Gary (*to Tom*) You did politics ay?

Tom Yes.

Gary Day you ken Sergei Nechayev?

Tom Is he from round here?

Eddie (*laughs*) Aye, he stays up the top ay the fucking toon.

Gary He was a Russian. (*Beat.*) Author ay *The Revolutionary Catechism*. (*Beat.*) One ay my heroes.

Eddie A top boy.

Gary Nechayev, Bakunin, Malatesta.

Eddie From a long line ay top boys.

Gary All advocates ay unconstitutional and non-parliamentary political activity ay one sort or another. (*Beat.*) Intellectual propaganda means nothing. (*Beat.*) Nay cunt listens tay a fucking debate. (*Beat.*) This is the propaganda ay the deed. (*Beat. Indicates Frank.*) He's a message.

Tom A message?

Gary That we've had enough.

Tom Enough what?

Gary Enough ay fucking everything. (*Pause. To Tom.*) It's kinday like when the natives in a Roman province would hay an uprising ay and like tay show their discontent they would attack the representatives ay the Romans ay Roman power ken imperial power. (*Beat.*) The propaganda ay the deed. (*Pause.*) They send these cunts . . . (*Indicates Frank.*) They come here all the time.

Eddie Burberry raincoat. Little suitcase on wheels. A couple ay wannabe types trailing along behind them. Curious about what sort ay dumb fuckers want tay work for them. (*Beat.*) He's probably doing a big report tay determine what factory, worldwide, has the biggest bunch ay widtinks staffing it. (*Beat.*) It's got tay be this one.

Pause.

Gary (*to Tom*) He was supposed tay be Japanese.

Tom Japanese.

Gary They're usually Japanese . . .

Eddie He'd ay been a much better representation ay a multinational corporation that way ken. (*Beat.*) But, hey, that's the nature ay the global economy, you dinnay ken who the fuck's in charge.

Pause.

Tom Where's he from?

Eddie (*takes security pass from his pocket*) Van de Hoy it says. What day you reckon? Dutch?

Tom Probably. (*Beat.*) Maybe Belgian. (*Beat.*) Flemish.

Eddie Right enough ay . . . Flemish. (*Pause.*) They're kinday unplaceable they cunts ay . . . that part ay Europe like . . . they're all big tall fuckers who speak ten languages.

Tom He's not very tall.

Pause.

Eddie No.

Pause.

Gary (*to Tom*) We're hoping he's American.

Pause.

Tom What are you going to do with the body?

Eddie Leave it here. Way a note. (*to Gary*) Did you day the note?

Pause. Gary takes a piece of paper from his pocket and hands it to Tom.

Tom (*reads it. To Gary*) What do you mean by precipitate?

Gary Well . . . ken . . . like . . . precipitation . . .

Eddie Is that no something tay day way rain.

Gary (*to Tom*) It's just an outline.

Tom It's quite vague.

Gary Of course it's vague . . . it's just tay give the media . . . an angle.

Tom (*pause. Reads it*) It's really vague.

Gary It's no that vague.

Eddie (*snatches piece of paper from Tom. Reads it. To Gary*) We've got tay make sure they get the right idea. Get them . . . on message.

Gary I ken. (*Pause.*) We can put ourselves forward for a quote . . . like when the telly and that are all over the place . . . point them in the right direction.

Pause.

Eddie That'll kinday blow our cover mind ay . . . appearing on the telly.

Tom You've really thought this through. I can see that.

Gary (*to Eddie*) Anonymous phone calls . . . tay newspapers. That's a better idea.

Tom It's all a bad idea.

Pause.

Gary (*to Tom*) You've got tay try and understand . . . ken . . . like him, (*indicating Frank*) people coming here . . . making decisions about me . . . about us . . .

Eddie It started tay get on our tits.

Gary You start thinking. About daying something.

Eddie You think mad thoughts when you're at your work.

Gary Mad fucking thoughts.

Pause.

Eddie (*to Tom*) It's no big deal. You can day anything now ay. Anything. Unlimited lifestyle choice. Whatever you want tay day in your spare time . . . you can day it. (*Beat.*) I've never been a political person. No till now. But I've always been interested in violence. Always . . . ken . . . really enjoyed it. (*Beat.*) I tried all the gratuitous stuff, the recreational violence ken, the leathering folk just for the sheer, amoral pleasure ay leathering them . . . and it was good at the time, dinnay get me wrong . . . but . . . ken the law ay diminishing marginal returns . . . it always kicks in eventually ay. (*Beat.*) Too many dysfunctional cunts involved tay ay. Too many cunts way problems. (*Beat.*) I thought . . . seen as how I'm a bit more mature now, seen as how I've advanced way beyond the point ay thinking going home to kick the loved ones in the puss is the path tay spiritual contentment, I thought I should maybe try something more idealistic, something way a point . . . see if that's what I needed. Ken . . . it's maybe more satisfying . . . violence way a reason. (*Beat.*) Gary here (*indicates Gary*) . . . he's always been a wee bit ay a political animal. We thought we'd put the two together and see if they still had a contribution tay make tay the modern workplace.

Gary (*to Tom*) See when I was a union rep all I ever got was fucking my pay's short, how can I no get my holidays when I want them, how am I no getting any overtime? I really wanted tay be out there blowing something up.

Tom I wish you had.

41

Eddie Blowing things up is difficult. It's a skilled trade. Humans are so much more accessible.

Gary It's a new era. (*Beat.*) People cannay help feeling it's a clean slate. Some things deserve another chance. (*Beat.*) Start ay the last century . . . big fucking upsurge in the anarchist violence. Sabotage. Assassinations. (*Beat.*) You never know, it could happen again.

Eddie (*indicating Frank*) He's an experiment.

Tom (*to Gary*) I thought you said he was a message?

Gary (*to Eddie*) He's a message.

Eddie He's an experiment tay.

Gary (*to Tom*) He'll give us an idea if there's a future in this. See if there's still a place for the big forces. (*Beat.*) It cannay be the end yet.

Eddie I fucking hope so. I'm no wasting my time on something way out a future.

Tom Perish the thought.

Gary (*to Tom*) You could be in at the start ay something big here.

Eddie We might make political violence fashionable again.

Gary This could provide answers.

Eddie (*to Tom*) Imagine if there's answers.

Pause.

Tom Something'll go wrong.

Gary Nothing'll go wrong.

Eddie (*to Tom*) I dinnay ken what your objection is? (*Beat.*) I hope it's no the moral aspect? There's nay morality involved.

Gary There are no innocents.

Pause.

Eddie (*to Tom*) What then? The polis?

Tom It had crossed my mind.

Eddie (*laughs*) Dinnay worry about them.

Gary The polis are fucking hopeless.

Tom They'll start with me.

Eddie You'll no say anything though.

Tom I'm a security guard. I'm supposed to notice what's going on.

Gary All you've got tay day is say you were sleeping. (*Beat.*) The worst they'll fucking day is sack you.

Eddie You keep saying you're fucking leaving anyway.

Gary What age are you?

Tom Twenty-two.

Gary Just finished your degree.

Tom Aye.

Gary Never been in trouble way the law before. (*Beat.*) You havenay have you?

Tom No.

Gary The police arenay gonnay seriously think a man ay your calibre would jeopardise everything by getting mixed up in something like this.

Pause.

Tom It's murder.

Pause.

Gary The way I see it is I've got nay fucking rights. Who the fuck woulday put up way this a hundred year ago. (*Pause.*) It's murder . . . but if they (*indicating Frank*) arenay gonnay be reasonable way us then why the fuck should we be reasonable way them?

Eddie (*puts his arm round Tom*) Dinnay worry about him. (*Indicates Frank.*)

Gary (*puts his arm round Tom from the other side*) Dinnay worry about your future.

Eddie Leave everything tay us.

Gary Keep calm.

Eddie Or I'll fucking shoot you tay.

   Pause.

Gary (*removes his arm from Tom and goes to Frank*) We should maybe try and wake him up.

Eddie (*to Gary*) Prod him.

Gary What?

Eddie Prod him.

   Gary prods Frank once.

Keep going. (*Removes his arm from Tom.*) You prod something . . . it's bound tay react eventually.

   Gary continues his prodding.

Tom (*to Gary*) You should chuck some water on him. (*Beat.*) I could go and get some from the canteen.

Eddie (*laughs. To Tom*) Ya cunt, they'd never have kept you in fucking Colditz ay? (*Beat.*) You keep coming up way plans like that and we'll put you in charge ay the escape committee.

Gary (*to Eddie*) It's no a bad idea though.

Eddie (*to Tom*) Keys.

Tom In my pocket.

Eddie (*takes the keys. Pulls out the gun. To Gary*) Are you wanting this?

Gary What for?

Eddie (*looks at Tom*) Aye . . . right enough.

    Eddie exits. Pause.

Tom How long have you known Eddie?

Gary Ever since I worked here.

    Pause.

Tom Is he . . . do you think . . . do you think he's . . . sane?

    Pause.

Gary I think . . . ken it would be easy tay say . . . ken, that he's mental. (*Beat.*) Really easy. (*Beat.*) Really fucking easy. (*Beat.*) But it wouldnay be right. (*Beat.*) Eddie . . . see . . . I think the thing is . . . his problem is . . . there's nothing fucked up in his background ken. He's no got anything tay be unhappy about, ken, no excuse. He should really be happy. (*Beat.*) Poor cunt. It must be a fucking nightmare. (*Beat.*) Me. (*Beat.*) I spend all my time working . . . all ay it. (*Beat.*) In here . . . Monday tay Friday, seven tay half two. (*Beat.*) I day weekend back shifts tay . . . flat rate, no overtime. (*Beat.*) Forty-nine hours a week in here. When I finish my back shifts on a Saturday and a Sunday I go straight fay here tay the hotel . . . the hotel (*indicating Frank*) he was staying in. (*Beat.*) I'm the weekend night porter . . . eleven till six in the morning. (*Beat.*) I finish on a

Monday and I'm straight back in here tay start my shift. (*Beat.*) I sometimes day the taxis tay. (*Beat.*) I'm fucking knackered. (*Beat.*) I cannay sleep . . . unless I'm pished. (*Beat.*) If I hadnay met that cunt . . . I dinnay ken. (*Pause.*) See when he came up way this idea, it was like . . . I could just feel like a weight coming off me . . . I got excited. I havnay been excited about anything for years.

Tom If it's excitement you want, why don't you just work for your brother?

Gary My brother. (*Pause.*) No. I'm an old-fashioned cunt. I dinnay agree way drugs. They're a waste ay time.

Tom It's where the money is.

Gary The money. (*Beat.*) The money's no anywhere round about here. The money's tucked up safe and sound in all they little screens in the City . . . buzzing about through the air. You should ken that. (*Beat.*) All them chinless merchant bankers . . . they must pish their pants at all the dumb fucks round here chopping each other up over ten-pound deals. A waste ay fucking time. (*Beat.*) No. (*Beat.*) The propaganda ay the deed. (*Pause.*) What would you day if you were me?

   Pause.

Tom I understand what you're talking about . . .

Gary Aye . . . but day you believe in it?

Tom It's not that I don't believe in it . . .

Gary You either believe in something or you dinnay.

Tom I think . . . a social conscience . . . it's a good thing. (*Beat.*) But . . . I want to get on.

Gary Get on?

Tom Have a career . . . do things.

Gary You're on one side or the other.

46

Tom It doesn't have to be like that any more . . .

Gary No?

Tom You don't have to choose. It doesn't have to be socialism or capitalism. You can pick what you want from both. Combine them.

Gary You cannay fucking combine them. (*Beat.*) That's just a fucking excuse for cunts who've sold out.

Tom You have to be on the inside to change things.

Gary But I'm no on the inside.

Tom You could be.

Gary (*laughs*) Right.

Tom You could.

Pause.

Gary No. (*Beat.*) It's too late for me.

Frank moves and lets out a moan.

Tom Shit.

Pause.

Gary You gonnay behave so I can tie him back up?

Tom (*holding out his tied hands*) No problems . . . I promise.

Gary begins to untie Tom.

It's not too late to stop this.

Gary Aye.

Tom You don't have to do it.

Gary I've got tay. (*Beat.*) I've got tay find out. (*Beat.*) Dinnay worry though . . . you'll be alright.

After freeing Tom, Gary begins to tie up Frank.

Tom (*indicating Frank*) Do you think he's got a family?

Gary Oh . . . aye . . . I dinnay ken ay. Never really thought about it ay.

Tom He's got a wedding ring on.

Eddie enters, carrying a mug.

Eddie Here we go. (*Holds up the mug.*) Freezing.

Gary Is that all you brought?

Eddie It was all I could find.

Gary That's no gonnay wake any cunt up.

Eddie In an ideal world I'd have liked a bucket ay . . .

Tom (*to Eddie. Points to Frank*) He's already moved.

Gary I told you he was alive.

Tom He sort of let out a groan.

Gary Just after you went.

Tom So we tied him back up.

Gary But he's gone a bit quiet again.

Tom At least he's alive.

Eddie No for fucking long he's no.

Eddie pours the water on Frank's face. Frank doesn't move.

Gary (*to Eddie*) See. No enough. Go and get more.

Tom You're going to need more than water.

Gary (*to Tom*) Give him a wee bit more time.

Frank moans and tries to lift his head.

See, he's getting better.

Frank's head drops and he goes still again.

Tom Much better.

Pause.

Eddie He does look a wee bit more conscious.

Tom How can you tell?

Eddie I dinnay ken. (*Beat.*) He looks less dead.

Gary (*to Frank*) Alright, pal.

Tom I don't think he'll be able to hear you.

Eddie (*loud. To Frank*) Alright.

Gary (*loud. To Frank*) Feeling better?

Tom He needs medical help.

Eddie (*shouts. To Frank*) How's the head?

Gary I'm sorry about your head and that.

Eddie He's (*indicating Gary*) . . . he's a wee bit enthusiastic.

Gary I dinnay really ken my own strength. (*Pause. To Eddie*) He can hear us.

Eddie (*to Gary*) I think he can like.

Tom He's totally out of it.

Eddie (*to Frank*) Can you hear me?

Tom He's probably got a fractured skull.

Frank moans and lifts his head.

Eddie (*to Tom*) See. (*Pulls Frank's security pass from his pocket and holds it in front of his face.*) Says here your name's Van de Hoy? Is that right ay?

Tom There's no point in asking him questions in that state.

Eddie (*to Frank*) It's your photo.

Frank mumbles incomprehensibly.

What was that?

Gary I dinnay ken.

Eddie I think it might ay been bring my boots, Marjory.

Gary (*to Frank*) What's your name?

Frank mumbles incomprehensibly.

(*to Frank*) Your name?

Frank mumbles incomprehensibly.

Eddie (*to Tom*) Did he say, can I have my wigwam up?

Gary (*holds the pass up to Frank's face*) Is that you?

Eddie Are you Van de Hoy?

Frank's head drops back on his chest.

Bastard. (*Pockets the pass. To Gary*) If you hadnay fucking half-killed him getting him here we coulday all been fucking home by now.

Gary Dinnay start fucking blaming me.

Tom (*to Gary*) Is it . . . like totally essential to talk to him . . . before . . .

Pause.

Eddie It's no . . . ken fucking totally essential ay . . .

Gary (*to Eddie*) Aye it fucking is. (*to Tom*) I want tay ask him a few things.

Tom What things?

Gary Just . . . things.

Tom See if he fits the mould.

Gary (*to Tom*) We've waited all this time . . .

Tom (*to Gary*) He's going to see you if he regains consciousness. You both know that don't you. (*Beat.*) He'll be able to identify you.

   Gary looks at Eddie.

Eddie (*to Tom*) I was supposed tay get balaclavas.

Gary But he didnay.

Eddie I tried.

Gary He decided we didnay need them.

Eddie (*to Gary*) You can only get woolly ones. (*to Tom.*) I'm allergic tay wool ay. (*Beat.*) It's no easy being a fucking terrorist when you're scratching your puss all the time.

Gary (*to Tom. Indicating Eddie*) He's allergic tay fucking everything him.

Eddie (*to Tom*) I am like. It's that anaphylactic shock shit ay. I can be killed by a peanut or a bee.

Tom Really?

Eddie Aye. (*Beat.*) So if you ever see a bee carrying a peanut, phone me.

   Pause.

Tom (*to Gary*) It's not too late. We can leave now.

Eddie Aye. Fuck it. (*Pulls the gun.*) I'll just kill him the now.

Tom (*to Eddie*) Hang on . . . I don't mean that.

Eddie Well what day you mean?

Tom I . . .

Eddie Well shut your puss then. (*Steps towards Frank.*)

Gary (*grabs Eddie's gun hand as he steps towards Frank*) We wait.

Eddie Aye?

Gary Aye.

Pause.

Eddie Aye, right enough ay . . . we might as well put him through a wee bit ay mental torture. (*Beat.*) I wouldnay mind doing the whole megalomaniac bit tay. Explain the plan for world domination and all that. (*Beat.*) I was quite looking forward tay that.

Frank (*raises his head*) World domination?

Gary (*startled*) Fucking hell.

Eddie You bastard.

Pause.

Gary (*to Frank*) How long have you been awake?

Eddie What did you fucking hear?

Frank (*to Eddie*) World domination?

Gary (*to Frank*) How long have you been listening?

Eddie Eavesdropping cunt.

Pause.

Tom (*to Frank*) How do you feel?

Eddie (*to Tom*) Shut it.

Pause.

Frank (*to Eddie*) Who are you?

Eddie I'm eh . . . I'm . . . doesnay matter who I am.

Pause.

Frank Where am I?

Eddie You're in Scotland.

Gary You're in Fife.   miserablism

Tom You're in Dunfermline.

Eddie You're in the shit.

Pause.

Gary (*to Frank*) You came here tay visit us . . .

Pause.

Frank (*to Gary*) Who are you?

Eddie Never mind who we are.

Gary (*to Frank*) I'm . . . the . . . the boy . . . I . . . we . . . we . . .

Tom (*to Eddie*) He doesn't sound very Dutch.

Eddie He doesnay, does he?

Gary No.

Eddie (*to Frank*) What fucking accent is that?

Gary What's that accent you've got? (*Pause.*) Are you American?

Tom He's not American.

Eddie United States.

Gary Please be American.

Pause.

Frank Why am I tied up?

Tom (*to Eddie*) He's definitely not American.

Gary Are you Dutch?

Eddie (*to Frank*) I thought you were Dutch . . . way the name and that. Flemish maybe.

Tom I said Flemish.

Gary (*to Frank*) You were supposed to be . . .

Tom Japanese.

   Pause.

Frank I'm not Japanese.

Eddie (*laughing*) Are you sure?

Gary They're usually . . .

Eddie Where are you from?

   Pause.

Frank Leven.

   Pause.

Gary Leven?

   Pause.

Tom (*laughs*) Leven. Fife

Eddie (*to Frank*) You're kidding me on ay?

Gary (*to Eddie*) Did he say Leven?

Eddie (*to Gary*) He said Leven.

Gary Fucking Leven.

Eddie The cunt.

Gary He cannay be fay Leven.

Tom (*to Gary*) That's what he said.

54

Eddie I'm gonnay fucking kill the cunt if he's fay fucking Leven. (*to Frank*) You're fucking dead if you're fay Leven.

Gary (*to Eddie*) He doesnay sound like he's fay Leven. (*to Frank*) You dinnay sound like you're fay Leven.

Frank Well I wouldn't . . . I haven't lived here for . . .

Eddie (*to Gary*) Let me kill him.

Frank . . . for years.

Pause.

Gary (*to Frank*) Where day you live now like?

Frank Surrey.

Gary Surrey.

Pause.

Frank Why am I tied up?

Tom You've been kidnapped.

Pause.

Frank I've been kidnapped.

Gary Aye.

Pause.

Frank Why?

Gary You're our boss.

Pause.

Frank Am I a hostage?

Eddie (*to Gary*) Now there's an idea.

Gary (*to Frank*) You're no a hostage.

Eddie (*to Frank*) How much day you think you're worth?

Frank I have a card in my wallet. There's a number on it. Phone the number.

Gary (*to Eddie*) He's no a hostage.

Eddie (*to Frank*) We didnay get your wallet. (*Holds up the pass.*) Just this.

Gary (*takes the pass. To Frank*) What's the F for?

Frank (*focuses on the pass*) The F?

Gary What's your name?

   Pause.

Frank Frank.

Gary Frank.

   Pause.

Frank If I'm not a hostage, why am I here?

Tom (*to Frank*) They're going to kill you.

Eddie Fuck's sake . . .

Tom (*to Eddie*) What?

Eddie You gonnay shut your puss?

Gary (*to Tom*) Aye. (*Beat.*) It's our fucking job tay tell the cunt what's happening.

Tom Sorry.

   Pause.

Frank (*to Gary*) You're going to kill me?

Gary Aye.

Eddie We . . . (*indicating Gary*) him and me . . . we're gonnay kill you.

Gary Aye.

  Pause.

Eddie (*to Frank*) Sorry and that like.

Frank Sorry?

Gary Aye.

Eddie It must come as a bit of a blow?

Frank Not really.

Eddie (*to Frank*) No really?

  Pause.

Gary (*to Frank*) It's a message . . . us killing you ken.

Frank A message?

Tom (*to Frank*) Or an experiment. Depends which one of these two you ask.

Eddie (*to Tom*) What the fuck did I just tell you?

  Pause.

Experiment.

Gary Message.

  Pause.

Frank (*to Gary*) So why haven't you?

Gary What?

Frank Killed me?

Gary I wanted tay talk tay you first.

Eddie (*to Frank*) He wants tay ken who he's killing.

Gary See what you think ay all this.

Pause.

Frank (*looks around at them*) I don't think very much of it.

Gary No. (*Indicates surroundings.*) This. What day you think ay this?

Pause.

Frank I . . .

Eddie Now before you start, I hope you're not one ay they fucking awful cunts that spouts all that corporate pish about how . . . you ken . . . how we're all part ay one big happy family. I hope you've never stood there and told the no-mark that cleans the bog he's just as important as the chief exec.

Gary I fucking hate cunts that day that. I hate it.

Eddie Makes my fucking skin crawl. (*Beat.*) I mean you're dead anyway . . . but I find it awfy difficult tay keep control ay myself when I hear that sort ay stuff.

Gary I'd rather you just took the pish.

Pause.

Frank I have . . . been known to . . . occasionally . . . I may have said things like that . . . once or twice . . . possibly . . .

Eddie (*to Gary*) I kent he'd be one ay they cunts. They're all like that.

Frank Always hoped someone would . . . call me . . . the . . . the fool I felt.

Gary (*to Frank*) Aye?

Eddie Aye right. Pish like that's no gonnay save you.

Frank (*to Eddie*) Maybe pish is all I've got.

Eddie Maybe.

Gary No. (*to Eddie*) Man like him . . . (*to Frank*) man like yourself . . . you must hay something. Got to. (*Pause. To Frank*) Day you no want tay tell us anything?

    Pause.

Frank (*to Gary*) You've decided who I am.

Gary No.

Frank Your minds are made up.

Gary Dinnay jump tay conclusions.

Frank My death is the conclusion.

Eddie Aye.

    Pause.

Frank (*to Gary*) Isn't it?

Eddie Aye.

    Pause.

Gary (*to Frank*) Just tell us a bit about yourself. (*Beat.*) Come on. Let's hear your story.

    Pause.

Frank Nothing much to tell. (*Beat.*) Always worked . . . until work brought me here.

    Pause.

Eddie (*to Frank*) Just like that? (*Beat.*) Nay effort or ambition or anything required? (*Beat.*) I'm following the same plan. What am I daying wrong?

    Pause.

Gary (*to Frank*) Day you enjoy it?

Frank (*to Gary*) It's work.

Gary It's work.

Frank Just work.

Gary What you day isnay work.

Pause.

How did you end up . . . working . . . for the Japs?

Frank I don't.

Gary Aye you day.

Frank This is an American company.

Gary No it's no.

Frank It was Japanese. But with all the problems in Asia . . . they've gradually been selling off anything that's . . . that's not a core business. (*Beat.*) You were acquired.

Eddie Bit of a shock that ay . . . what happened in Japan.

Frank They'll be back.

Eddie Aye.

Pause.

Gary So what day you day for this American mob?

Frank I'm a consultant.

Gary So what are they consulting you about?

Frank They just want me to have . . . just have a look around . . . see what's viable.

Gary (*to Frank*) Is this place gonnay shut?

Frank It's very early . . .

Eddie Dinnay worry, we're no bothered about that. There's plenty shite jobs floating about.

Tom We're spoilt for choice.

Eddie We ken you're only here 'cause we're cheap.

Gary Tell us. (*Beat.*) Tell us if it is.

Eddie Capital comes, capital goes. That's the nature ay capital. Nay cunt's fucking immune ay. Got tay consider the options provided globally for inward investment. There's always some mob ay peasants scratching at the topsoil somewhere whose wildest dream is a shift in here.

Gary That place you've got in Mexico . . . they're always going on about there . . . what day you pay them?

Frank I don't pay them.

Gary Well what does the company pay them?

Frank What they're worth.

Gary What they're fucking worth?

Tom (*to Gary*) It's economics.

Gary Well, I dinnay ken much about economics, but I ken what I like . . . and it isnay fucking that.

Eddie Mexico. (*Beat. To Frank*) You'll no even need fire exits over there.

    Pause.

Tom So you travel a lot?

    Pause.

Frank Travel's part of business.

Gary (*to Frank*) You learned anything on your travels? Apart fay where's cheapest.

Pause.

Tom (*to Frank*) Eastern Europe's cheap.

Frank Everywhere in the East is cheap. (*Beat.*) The whole world's moving East.

Pause.

Tom (*to Frank*) I was reading this thing in a magazine a while ago . . . it was about this thing called the Golden Banana.

Eddie (*to Tom*) A dirty mag like?

Tom No. (*to Frank*) Have you heard of it?

Frank No.

Tom It's the area of Europe which is going to get the most economic development and prosperity in the future.

Eddie That's a good name like . . . the Golden Banana. I like when they give places daft names like that.

Pause.

Tom Bristol to Barcelona . . . that's the area it's gonnay cover apparently . . . this banana.

Eddie I can see how that might work . . . banana-wise like.

Gary (*to Tom*) There wasnay any mention ay us?

Tom No.

Eddie Mightay fucking known ay.

Pause.

Tom (*to Frank*) Prague's nice. (*Beat.*) If you ever end up in Eastern Europe. (*Beat.*) I've been to Prague.

Frank It is, isn't it?

Tom Beautiful.

Frank Budapest too.

Tom Never been.

Frank Lovely.

Eddie (*to Tom*) Dinnay you be fucking bonding now.

Tom I'm not bonding . . . I'm just chatting.

Eddie Whatever you're doing . . . stop it. (*to Frank*) It's one ay the major occupational hazards ay kidnapping that . . . bonds forming leads tay all sorts ay problems.

Tom I'm not bonding. I'm just talking . . . about Prague.

Eddie Well stop fucking talking about fucking Prague.

   Pause.

Gary (*to Tom*) Too many tourists in Prague. They'll no be interested in this sort ay work. (*Beat.*) They'll go somewhere . . . but it'll no be anywhere you go for a holiday.

Eddie Good fucking riddance. Give them a few years ay working for these cunts and they'll be screaming for the Russians back. (*Beat.*) There's an idea. (*to Frank*) You could move this place to Russia. Russians'll day fucking anything. (*Beat.*) If you dinnay get a fatal dose ay radiation every time you turn up for your shift it's a bonus over there. Child labourers ten a penny, eat dirt, live in sewers. (*Beat.*) Or is that Romania?

Tom I thought it was Brazil.

Gary No. It's definitely Russia.

Eddie Russia ay. Whatever happened tay Russia?

Frank They lost. (*Pause.*) Russia seems to go from one dark age to another.

Gary What's so wrong way the dark ages?

Frank Lack of light.

Pause.

Gary (*to Frank*) We've got a bit ay a communist tradition round here you ken.

Eddie We're very political. (*Beat.*) He's (*indicates Tom*) got a degree in it. (*Beat.*) In fact . . . (*to Frank*) have you no got any vacancies for a bright-eyed, bushy-tailed, keen-as-mustard youngster way a dodgy degree? (*to Tom*) Come on . . . sell yourself.

Frank I can't give him a job if you kill me.

Eddie Right enough ay. (*to Tom*) Oh well . . . too bad. (*to Frank*) He secretly quite likes the uniform anyway.

Pause.

Frank (*to Tom*) What made you do politics?

Tom I'm . . . interested in it.

Eddie (*pulls out the gun*) You dinnay seem very interested now.

Tom This isn't politics.

Eddie This is politics alright.

Gary (*to Gary*) We talked about getting a politician ay. Nay fucking point. (*to Tom*) These cunts (*indicating Frank*) are are in charge. Dinnay fucking kid yourself. Politicians don't matter a fuck any more. You could shoot fifty fucking MPs. Nay cunt gives a fuck. Kill this cunt and every cunt'll wonder why. They (*indicating Frank*) hold absolute power in the world.

Eddie This is fucking politics alright. (*Flourishes the firearm.*) This is the best type ay politics. (*Beat.*) And while we're on the subject . . . (*to Frank*) when day I get my fucking oil rig?

Pause.

Frank I'm sorry . . . I . . .

Eddie I mean can anycunt tell me?

Pause.

Gary (*to Eddie*) What the fuck are you on about?

Eddie When day I get my oil rig?

Pause.

Tom Your oil rig?

Eddie Aye. My oil rig. Ken . . . fay the new parliament. The one they're building. The one that's gonnay give us (*shouting in Braveheart style*) freedom. When day they cunts start divvying up the crude? That's been what? Two? Three year? Havenay even had as much as a fucking barrel. (*Strikes more poses with the gun. To Gary*) Have you had a shot?

Gary I'm alright.

Eddie (*more poses*) You've got tay hay a shot like.

Gary Aye.

Eddie Never had a shot ay a gun before. (*Beat.*) Have you?

Gary No . . . aye . . . well . . . never fired one ay.

Eddie Gives you a right feeling ay . . . power.

Pause.

Frank (*to Eddie*) Hitting the target. (*Beat.*) That's the difficult part. (*Beat.*) When you're not used to it.

Eddie Aye. (*Points the gun at Frank*.) I think I'll manage. (*to Frank*) Ever had a shot ay one ay these?

Frank Oh yes.

Eddie Aye?

Frank Yes.

   Pause.

Eddie Manage to hit your target?

Frank Always.

   Pause.

Eddie (*to Tom*) What about you?

Tom No.

Eddie You should hay a shot like. (*Offers the gun.*)

Gary (*to Eddie*) Dinnay give him it.

Eddie Oh aye . . . right enough ay. (*to Tom*) Dinnay want you making any citizen's arrests. (*Beat.*) What sort ay powers does that uniform give you anyway?

Tom I think I can search your bags when you leave the building.

Eddie Now that's what I call power. (*Eddie twirls the gun round his finger.*)

Gary (*to Eddie*) Stop mucking about way that.

   Eddie puts the gun in the waistband of his trousers.

(*to Eddie*) You better no be on something.

Eddie Just high on life, neebur.

Gary I mean it.

Eddie I'm alright. (*Beat.*) You ken I've knocked all that on the head ay. (*to Tom*) Wasnay agreeing way me any more . . . the powders and the pills.

Tom Too much of a payback.

Eddie It wasnay so much the payback . . . more the actual effect.

Gary (*to Tom*) Nothing in moderation. That's his rule.

Eddie I had tay take that much tay get anything off it ay.

Frank (*to Eddie*) Psychotic episodes?

Pause.

Eddie The psychotic episodes were fuck all. After a while you get tay know your psychotic episodes . . . it was the rectal prolapses were the nightmare. It's bad enough thinking every cunt's after you but when you're actually shitting yourself tay. (*Beat.*) I stopped all ay it . . . drink tay . . . well I stopped drinking as much. (*Beat.*) I mean you cannay stop drinking totally, can you? That would be fucking sick. (*Takes a deep breath.*) Never felt fucking better. (*to Gary. Indicating Frank*) I thought we were gonnay torture him?

Pause.

Tom (*to Frank*) Do you . . . do you, you know . . . think that devolution's been a success?

Pause.

Frank (*looks at Eddie and Gary*) Obviously not.

Gary (*to Tom*) He doesnay live here . . . so it's got fuck all tay day way him. (*to Frank*) Ay?

Pause.

Frank (*to Tom*) You said you had a degree in politics?

Tom Yes.

Frank What were you interested in?

Tom All the . . . like . . . the left-wing stuff, labour relations, things like that. (*Beat.*) My grandad was a miner.

Frank My father was a miner.

Gary My father and my grandfather were miners. (*Pause. To Tom*) Where was your grandad fay?

Tom Lumphinnans.

Eddie The Soviet Socialist Republic ay Lumphinnans.

Gary Nay shite?

Tom Aye. beginning to imitate Eddie

Gary Mine's was fay Cowdenbeath. They maybe kent each other . . . every fucker ay that age kens each other ay.

Eddie (*laughs*) You're maybe cock-related.

Gary My grandad was a communist. Right intay the union and that ay. He went tay the Spanish Civil War.

Tom Aye?

Gary He was some cunt like.

Tom That's pretty impressive . . . going tay Spain.

Eddie I've been tay Spain loads ay times.

Frank (*to Tom*) There was quite a few from round here who joined the International Brigades.

Tom Yes.

Gary Fucking heroes.

   Pause.

Tom I did my dissertation on working-class militancy in Lumphinnans in the inter-war years.

Gary It was one of the Little Moscows. One of the most radical places in Britain in the twenties and thirties. A place in Wales. Mardy. And Lumphinnans.

Eddie Little fucking Moscow . . . Lumphinnans. (*Beat.*) Mind you . . . nothing in the shops . . . crime . . . suppose it's quite like Moscow.

Gary In the nineteen twenty-one lockout Fife stayed out longer than anyone else.

Frank They always did.

Gary And in the General Strike . . .

Eddie They were still out fay nineteen twenty-one. (*to Gary*) Fucking listen tay you. (*Beat.*) That shite's all dead and buried. It's no the fucking twenties any more.

Tom What about the strike in eighty-four?

Eddie Seventeen year ago. Different fucking world.

Gary Stayed out for a year.

Eddie For fucking what? (*Beat.*) Twelve months ay free school meals for their bairns.

Gary There's a tradition here.

Eddie Tradition.

Gary It's our duty to be . . .

Eddie Mental.

Gary To remember.

   Pause.

Tom (*to Frank*) There's a street called Gagarin Way in Lumphinnans.

Frank Is there?

Gary Yuri Gagarin. The astronaut.

Frank Cosmonaut.

Gary Ay?

Frank (*to Gary*) The Soviets called them cosmonauts. (*Pause.*) The twelfth of April, nineteen sixty-one.

Gary (*to Frank*) Ay?

Frank (*to Gary*) The twelfth of April, nineteen sixty-one. (*Beat.*) The date that Yuri Alekseyevich Gagarin orbited the earth. (*Pause.*) It was my sixteenth birthday.

Eddie Aye? (*Beat.*) Ya cunt, how the fuck did your mum manage tay arrange that?

   Pause.

Tom (*to Frank*) It shows the influence though. (*Beat.*) Doesn't it?

Frank Influence?

Gary Of communism.

Frank Does it?

Tom Why Gagarin Way . . . if it isn't?

Eddie First primate way a surname in space.

Gary First Soviet in space.

Eddie Gagarin Way. (*Beat.*) Armstrong Road. (*Beat.*) Aldrin Avenue. They'll be fucking everywhere.

Gary First Soviet in space.

Tom (*to Eddie*) Why else would they do it?

Eddie Well, never having known the spiritual communion ay squatting underground in the dark, hacking at a two-inch seam, I dinnay think I'm qualified tay comment on their motivation. (*Beat.*) But I suppose . . . when the sputnik went up the locals thought we werenay far away fay worldwide Soviet domination . . . they've thought, ya cunt, we better get a street named after one ay them before the Red Army rolls in and starts whacking suspected capitalist collaborators.

Gary (*to Tom*) They did it because he was a hero of the Soviet Union.

Eddie They backed the wrong fucking horse.

Pause.

Frank The wrong horse. (*to Tom*) Was that your conclusion?

Pause.

Tom When I was doing it . . . the dissertation . . . I went . . . I arranged this interview . . . up in Cowdenbeath, in this sheltered housing place, with a few of these old union guys. I thought they were all going to be like Joe Stalin's best mates.

Frank Joe Stalin killed all his best mates.

Tom I'm talking to all these old guys and I start being like all professorial . . . like . . . saying to them, do you not hold that much of the radicalism of the miners grew from the fact that they were forced to work underground and were therefore further alienated by the oppressive nature of the darkness . . . They all just looked at me like I'm daft . . . one of them goes, no, son, you have to go underground, that's where the coal is. (*Beat.*) I felt a right idiot. (*Beat.*) There was this other bloke who told me he got blacklisted from the pits . . . I said, were you victimised because of your political activities? . . . He goes, no, I hit the foreman over the head with a shovel for shagging my wife.

Pause.

Eddie A lot ay cunts make the mistake ay thinking there's some underclass out there . . . sitting about . . .

ripe for rebellion. All they're fucking ripe for is getting the right six numbers on a Saturday night.

Gary They have to be provoked.

Pause.

Frank (*to Gary*) Your grandad. (*Beat.*) Did he ever tell you what actually happened in Spain?

Gary No really. (*Beat.*) He was a bit ay an adventurer ken . . . at the Somme at sixteen . . . lied about his age so he could join up. (*Beat.*) I never really knew him.

Frank In Spain . . . once they knew they were beat . . . they turned on one another . . . the forces of the left.

Gary He never really talked about it ay. By the time I came along he was an old man. (*Pause.*) People arenay the same any more.

Pause.

Tom The Somme was mad.

Eddie There were loads ay mad battles.

Frank Everything was different after the Somme.

Eddie That was the poets' fault. All that fuckin' cannon-fodder poignancy . . . it appeals tay poets ken . . . the whole 'ours is not tay reason why, ours is tay jump out ay the trench and walk very slowly towards the machine guns'. Doesnay make good films like . . . but the poets love it. (*Beat.*) The Second World War killed loads more but there's like this rosy glow about it.

Tom Aye, all they old folk who cannay get enough ay the Blitz.

Frank Happiest days of their lives.

Pause.

Gary (*to Eddie*) Mind when I was on holiday a couple ay year ago . . . way the wife and bairns and that.

Eddie Flamingoland.

Gary Flamingoland.

Tom Flamingoland?

Gary (*to Tom*) It's near Scarborough.

Tom Are there flamingos?

Gary A few concrete ones.

Eddie (*to Tom*) I suppose you wouldnay go near a place like that ay. (*to Frank*) He's a cunting backpacker.

Tom I just wondered why they called it Flamingoland.

Eddie Tay give it some sort ay connection way a hot, exotic location like fucking Florida or something ay.

Frank (*to Tom*) They can't call it Disneyland, they'd get sued.

Gary Is no cunt gonnay listen tay me?

Eddie Aye.

Frank Sorry.

Tom Go on.

Gary (*to Tom*) So we're in this fucking Flamingoland ay . . . and like . . . ken I decides tay hay a wee bit ay an explore. I says tay the wife I'll give her a break fay the bairns. I loads them in the car and we fuck off. I'm driving about . . . braw day . . . fucking scorching . . . and I get stuck behind this fucking coach . . . follows it for a bit and it like pulls in tay this place. I think well it must be somewhere . . . ken something tay day . . . in I goes . . . in the car park. Unbecuntinlievable. Total fucking old cunts convention . . . the whole place fucking stowed . . . coaches ay them. Wheelchairs, crutches, zimmers, the fucking lot.

Tom (*to Gary*) What was it?

Gary Ken . . . what you were saying . . . like the fucking Blitz Experience ken, like a theme park.

Tom You're joking. (*to Eddie*) Really?

Eddie I've seen the photos.

Gary Total fucking walk through and it's all piles ay rubble way bairns' hands sticking out.

Tom No.

Gary Way like little fucking robot voices crying and screaming and shouting for help and that ken.

Gary And it's really fucking loud ay, cause they're all fucking deaf. They even had a fucking underground way like chirpy cockney robots lying in it, sleeping and that ay.

Eddie Singing defiant songs around the old joanna.

Gary And at the end there was this like theatre way ken all Vera Lynn impersonators and that coming out and singing fucking 'We'll Meet Again'.

Tom Unbelievable.

Gary The codgers were going bonkers . . . jumping out the wheelchairs and that . . . dancing.

Tom Amazing.

Gary Six-fifty a skull tay see something you've already lived through. Ay? (*Beat.*) Paying money tay some cunt so you can go home and wake up fucking screaming when the nightmares come back. (*Beat.*) What the fuck's that all about?

Frank Happiest days of their lives.

Pause.

Gary We'll have nothing tay go on about when we're old.

Eddie (*to Gary*) What about this? (*Pause. To Frank*) I've got tay say like . . . I'm quite looking forward tay being an old cunt.

Frank Are you?

Eddie Especially the Alzheimer's and that ay. (*Beat.*) Ken, parading about in the buff and that ay. (*to Tom*) You should get in tay the Alzheimer game like . . . nursing homes and that ay. That's the fucking industry ay the future. (*Beat.*) Gonnay be nothing but old folk soon. Way loads ay fucking money and no fucking idea how they got it. (*Beat*) These places . . . ken like old factories and that . . . they'd be perfect. (*Beat.*) When this lot fuck off tay China, get in, snap this place up on the cheap, fill it full ay bunk beds and battery-farm the old cunts.

Tom You'd get thousands in a place this size.

Pause.

Eddie It was better when you just had tay day the contracted three score and ten ay. (*Beat.*) I mean they slag the cuisine ay Scotland but at least it kept the pension spending down. You eat a fried breakfast and a fish supper a day and you're guaranteed tay keel over a couple ay days after retiring. (*Beat.*) It's the perfect fucking system. I dinnay ken why they bother way this healthy eating pish. (*Beat.*) And at least dropping dead at sixty-five fay a massive fucking coronary thrombosis leaves you way a wee bit ay dignity ay. At least the nearest and dearest get tay remember a laughing, talking, smoking, drinking, meat-pie-eating human being ay. They dinnay get the golden fucking memory ay the loved one idling away their dotage in some cunt else's pish-soaked clothes.

Pause.

Gary I'm no gonnay let myself get in that state.

Tom By the time we get to that age we'll be able to get an injection . . . on the continent . . . or in the post or something.

Eddie Or as like part ay a holiday. Take the family along, blow all their inheritance and on the last day ay the fortnight . . . (*Mimes an injection.*)

Tom I think you can get euthanasia in Amsterdam.

Eddie There's a shock.

Tom It's legal in certain circumstances.

Eddie Maybe the ferries'll start a special trip. The euthanasia special. Two seats going, one coming back, coffin on the fucking roof rack.

Pause.

Tom (*to Frank*) Have you got a family?

Frank Yes.

Tom (*to Gary*) He's got a family.

Gary Aye. (*Pause. To Frank*) I'll admit it right . . . when we came up way this idea . . . it didnay occur tay me about your family . . .

Eddie It's our first time at this ken . . . we'll get better.

Pause.

Gary I'm sure they'll be alright . . . your family ken . . . your kids . . . if you've got any?

Pause.

Frank I don't really see much of them. My children. My wife and I split up . . . well . . . quite a few years ago now . . . and . . . well I haven't . . . I don't see a great deal of them.

Tom You must miss them?

Frank Only when I'm awake.

Eddie (*to Frank*) Dinnay you worry. They'll be fine. (*Beat.*) I'm sure they'll all go on tay hold senior management positions in some big company . . . jetting here and there . . . attracting the resentment ay the embittered dossers who work for them. (*Beat.*) Chip off the old block.

Pause.

Frank My son's a . . . he's part of a . . . a group of travellers.

Pause.

Gary Travellers?

Eddie (*laughs*) Is he a tree-hugger?

Frank I don't know. (*Beat.*) He lives on a bus.

Pause.

Gary A bus?

Frank Yes.

Pause.

Gary Fuck's sake.

Pause.

Eddie (*to Frank*) Is it a double-decker?

Frank I don't know. (*Pause.*) Why?

Eddie I was just thinking . . . ken . . . it's maybe the size ay your bus that, ken determines your status in the . . . in the tribe. (*Beat.*) He's maybe doing no bad for himself. He's maybe king ay the buses.

   Pause.

Gary I dinnay ken any cunt who lives on a bus.

Eddie (*to Frank*) That's what you get for bringing them up in Surrey.

Gary What's living on a bus gonnay day . . . ay? (*Beat.*) Pointless. Fucking pointless. (*Beat.*) You have tay hay a job. The only way tay stop . . . tay oppose capitalist society . . . is tay work. You threaten nay cunt sitting in a lay-by. Workers control the economic power. (*to Frank*) I tell them that but they dinnay seem tay realise. They're no interested in organising. (*to Frank*) You've kinday been unlucky. (*Beat.*) We . . . I . . . I never imagined . . . doing this ay . . . I could never have imagined. (*Beat.*) Methods grow out ay their environment. Where apathy's at its greatest you have tay outrage the greatest. (*Beat.*) Killing you's a last resort. (*Beat.*) Syndicalism would be my choice.

Frank You're anarchists?

Gary We're workers.

Frank Never really caught on here. (*Beat.*) Anarchism.

Gary We're the centre ay economic activity.

Frank More a Latin thing. Spain and Italy.

Gary We're the most powerful people in this country.

Frank Perhaps you need hot blood. (*Beat.*) I understand the emotional appeal of anarchism. It's always appealed

to artists, people who are interested in ideas. (*Beat.*)
Always appealed to impressionable minds. (*Beat.*)
Anarchism's always at its most popular when another
socialist movement has failed. (*to Gary*) It's at its most
popular during non-revolutionary periods. (*Beat.*)
Stability, that's what leads to an interest in anarchy.
That's why they're so passionate . . . the only other thing
they can do . . . is give up the hope of revolution.

Gary No.

Pause.

Frank (*to Gary*) You think you can find answers in the
past?

Gary You've got tay look for them somewhere.

Frank Well the past should have taught you one thing.

Gary What?

Frank You don't live in a revolutionary society.

Pause.

Eddie (*to Frank*) I'm no a fucking anarchist. (*Beat.*)
I dinnay like labels. No unless they're on my clothes.
(*Beat.*) And I'm quite partial tay a Big Mac. Which
kinday disqualifies me fay the anarchist movement.
(*Beat.*) They should maybe start doing anarchist happy
meals ay . . . McDonalds . . . stop the cunts smashing
their fucking windows.

Pause.

Frank (*to Eddie*) So why are you here?

Eddie Well I've kinday been outflanked by the fluid
nature ay modern demographics . . . have you not heard
there's a crisis in masculinity at the moment. (*Beat.*)
We're finding it difficult. (*to Gary*) Aren't we? (*Pause.*)

I might as well cause a wee bit ay havoc while I adjust. (*Beat.*) And it's something tay day when the telly's pish. (*Beat.*) I'm a troublemaker . . . I like causing trouble. It's my hobby. (*Beat.*) I think it's important tay have a hobby . . . keeps you out ay trouble.

Gary (*to Frank*) It's no a hobby.

Frank (*to Eddie*) You want to kill me as a hobby?

Eddie I just want tay kill you. (*Beat.*) For me.

Gary (*to Frank*) It's no a fucking hobby.

Eddie Here we cunting go.

Gary (*to Frank*) It only takes a few folk tay show the way forward. A handful ay individuals.

Eddie (*to Frank*) Cannay kill anycunt without making a fucking speech.

Gary (*to Frank*) Twenty year ago nay cunt would ay put up way the pish we have tay in here. A hundred year ago they'd ay burnt the fucking place down.

Eddie (*to Frank*) That's fay the heart like. That's real.

Gary If I put up way it then I'm a fucking, spineless bastard . . . and I'm no.

Eddie (*to Frank*) He's a vertebrate.

Gary (*to Eddie*) Fuck off.

  Pause.

Eddie (*to Frank*) I cannay match that level ay commitment. It's way beyond me. (*Beat.*) I can pay lip service tay it like . . . but I only day shallow. (*Beat.*) But dinnay think for a minute that I dinnay take my shallow seriously.

  Pause.

Frank You wouldn't have let me see your faces if you weren't serious.

Eddie looks at Gary. Pause.

(*to Tom*) What about you, son?

Tom It's nothing to do with me.

Frank Why are you here?

Tom My hat . . .

Gary (*to Frank*) It was a mistake.

Tom I thought they were just stealing.

Eddie (*to Frank*) He opened the gate.

Tom I didn't know they were going to . . .

Frank Kill me.

Pause.

Tom I didn't know.

Pause.

Frank (*to Tom*) You don't agree with this then? (*Pause. To Tom*) Well, do you?

Tom I didn't know.

Frank I didn't ask you that.

Pause.

Tom I just think there's other ways.

Frank Other ways.

Tom To achieve what they want.

Gary (*to Frank*) It's nothing tay day way him.

Pause.

Frank (*to Tom*) So . . . you just walk out of here after they've killed me?

Gary (*to Frank*) He'll be alright. It's nothing tay day with him.

Frank (*to Tom*) You think they're going to let you go . . . you're a witness.

Gary (*to Frank*) He's alright. (*Beat.*) He's no the enemy.

Frank Are you sure?

Pause.

Tom (*to Frank*) I wish I wasn't here . . .

Eddie (*to Frank*) He wishes he was back at university, all nice and safe fay the real world.

Pause.

Gary You'll be a graduate ay?

Frank (*to Tom*) I was at university in nineteen sixty-eight. There were huge demonstrations then.

Eddie Did a couple ay students no get tear-gassed in Paris or something?

Frank A couple of students?

Eddie They like a riot in France ay. (*Beat.*) Scarf round the puss, hip-hop soundtrack.

Pause.

Tom (*to Frank*) Were you there?

Frank In Paris? (*Beat.*) No. I was in London. At the LSE. There were occupations there. The Situationists. (*Laughs.*) They were anarchists.

Gary (*to Frank*) But it was fuck all . . . I mean it wasnay a revolution . . . it was students . . . fucking middle-class hippies having a laugh . . . it's workers cause revolutions.

Pause.

I was at the poll-tax riot.

Tom Really?

Gary Oh aye.

Eddie (*to Tom*) Lucky bastard ay.

Gary Best day ay my life.

Eddie They should let folk ken when it's really gonnay go off like that . . . ken . . . so no cunt misses out.

Tom (*to Gary*) Was it good?

Gary Good? (*Beat.*) I went banzai. Middle ay Trafalgar Square . . . fucking throwing everything . . . everything I could get my hands on.

Eddie (*to Tom*) I was at a soul weekender in Southport. (*Beat.*) I can mind Tim Westwood arrived late for his spot and starts going on about how the streets are on fire . . . every cunt was like . . . shut your puss and get some records on.

Gary (*to Frank*) See? (*indicating Eddie*) Dancing instead ay rioting.

Eddie It was a good weekender.

Gary I try to tell them. We've wasted so much time.

Eddie (*to Gary*) I'm here now.

Gary Given away so much.

Eddie Is that no enough?

Gary Been distracted so much.

Eddie It's no just my fault.

Gary They're so easily distracted.

Eddie It's no just my fault . . . it's everycunt's fault. (*Beat.*) My fault, (*pointing to Gary*) your fault, (*pointing to Tom*) his fault, (*pointing to Frank*) and his fault. Everycunt's fault. I'm here now. Let's get on way it. (*Drags Frank from his seat and forces him to kneel.*)

Gary (*to Eddie*) I need tay find out more.

Eddie The talking's over. No more distractions.

Tom (*to Eddie*) You can't do this.

Eddie Watch me.

Gary (*to Frank*) Have you nothing else tay say?

Frank What's there to say?

Gary I need tay know more about you.

Eddie (*to Gary*) We ken he's no the type for breaking down at least ay.

Frank What would be the point?

Tom (*to Eddie*) There's another way to do this.

Eddie Is there?

Tom You said it yourself. Unlimited choice. We can do anything we want.

Eddie And I want tay day this.

   Pause.

Tom (*to Gary*) And what do you want?

Eddie He wants tay day this too.

Tom (*to Gary*) Do you? (*Beat.*) Gary?

Eddie Aye.

Tom (*to Eddie*) We were talking about this earlier . . . weren't we, Gary?

Eddie (*to Gary*) You're becoming quite friendly, you two, ay.

Tom I was saying how you don't need to take sides now. (*Beat.*) The economy . . . capitalism . . . it's not an end in itself . . . it's a tool. We can use it.

    Frank laughs.

Tom It doesn't have to be one or the other, socialism or capitalism. (*Beat.*) It can be both.

    Pause.

Eddie (*to Tom*) You know . . . see since I got here tonight, you've been hanging about and getting in the way and . . . like, at one point, I was kinday wishing it was you that I had tay kill. (*Lets go of Frank and moves towards Tom.*) But you're right . . . I just realised . . . just now . . . what you said. (*Puts a hand on Tom's shoulder.*) There is another way tay day this. (*Hits Tom over the head with the gun.*) Without you fucking annoying me.

Gary What did you day that for?

Eddie I've had enough ay him. (*Beat.*) Nay witnesses tay. (*Returns to Frank.*) Everybody's said their piece.

Gary There must be . . . more.

Eddie All the avenues have been explored.

Gary (*to Frank*) I need tay ken. (*Pause. To Frank*) Answer me.

Frank I'm not very good at answers.

Eddie (*holds up the gun*) I've got the answers.

Gary Why won't you defend yourself?

    Pause.

Frank It's been a long day.

Eddie (*puts the gun against Frank's head*) The day's over.

Gary (*to Frank*) Why won't you defend what you day?

Frank I don't have to defend what I do. (*Beat.*) What I do defends itself. Always has, always will. (*Beat.*) Your . . . workers . . . they think because they're not underground . . . because they're not covered in shit . . . they think they've gone up in the world. All they want is to own things, doesn't matter what it is, any shite'll do, so long as it's theirs. (*Beat.*) Give the natives a few shiny beads and they'll be happy. If they get a bit restless, make the next bead a wee bit shinier.

Eddie (*to Gary*) He's good. (*to Frank*) Are we related?

Frank He . . . (*indicating Tom*) silly cunt . . . he thinks capitalism can be domesticated . . . (*Laughs. Pause.*) They don't realise how powerless they are. (*to Gary*) They don't understand . . . and you won't make them. (*Pause.*) But . . . if you want someone who's easier to kill? (*Beat.*) If you want me to say I've exploited and robbed honest, working people? Caused my fair share of suffering? Destroyed the environment? Fine. I've done it. So has everybody else. You want arrogance? Greed? Stupidity? Look around. There's no need for defences when something's everywhere. (*Pause. To Gary*) That's why you're beat. I dinnay hay tay defend anything. (*Beat.*) And I'll tell you another thing, pal . . . and this I day ken. (*Beat.*) You're no a fucking threat . . . you're no even an alternative. (*Beat.*) I'll no be missed. I'm fifty-fucking-six. I'm over. (*Beat.*) Had enough ay trailing round the world. Seen enough fucking airports. Paid enough fucking hookers. (*Beat.*) Get on with it. I've had enough ay this fucking shite.

Eddie Aye, me fucking tay.

Gary (*to Frank*) But if you willnay defend yourself . . . (*Pause. To Eddie*) We cannay kill him.

Eddie Ay?

Gary It willnay mean anything.

Eddie (*to Gary*) It means fuck all anyway. Have you no been fucking listening?

Gary It cannay mean nothing . . .

Eddie (*to Gary*) Listen . . . just because he doesnay fit your preconceived idea ay a robber baron doesnay mean I cannay have my fucking fun.

Gary (*to Eddie*) You cannay kill him.

Eddie (*cocks the gun and puts it against Frank's head*) Bye.

Gary (*to Frank*) Just tell me . . . tell me one fucking thing. (*Pause.*) What would you day if you were me?

   Pause.

Frank Get on with it.

Eddie Well fucking said. (*Pulls the trigger. There is a click.*) Fuck. (*Pulls the trigger again. The same click.*) Fuck's sake. (*Pulls the trigger again. The same click.*) What's fucking going on?

Gary You cannay kill him.

Eddie (*examines the gun. To Gary*) What's wrong way this?

Gary There's like . . . nay bullets ay.

Eddie Nay bullets?

Gary Aye.

Eddie How?

Gary They're extra.

Eddie Extra?

Gary Extra money.

Eddie And? (*Beat.*) Did we no have enough money?

Gary Aye . . . but . . . they wouldnay have given me the gun if they thought we were gonnay fire it.

Eddie Is that no the point ay a fucking gun . . . firing it?

Gary They have tay get rid ay it if you fire it.

Eddie I dinnay believe this like.

Gary You cannay just start spraying bullets about. (*Beat.*) This isnay America.

   Pause.

Eddie This is . . . so . . . fucking . . . unprofessional.

Frank That's anarchism for you. (*Eddie hits Frank with the gun. To Gary*) You might ay fucking told me.

Gary I was waiting for my moment. (*Beat.*) I was ken . . . like gonnay pull you aside ay.

   Pause.

Eddie (*pulls out a knife*) Good job I've got this then. (*Stabs Frank.*) Tried and trusted. (*Stabs Frank.*) Traditional. (*Stabs Frank.*) If you don't keep the old traditions going the young'll forget. (*Stabs Frank.*) Then where'll we be?

   Pause.

Gary (*kneels beside the body. To Eddie*) He's dead.

Eddie Funny that. (*to Gary*) I thought that was the point. (*Pause. Looking at the blood on the knife and his*

hands and clothes) State ay me. (*Points to his jacket.*)
This is fucking new. (*Beat. To Frank*) Cunt. (*Laughs.*)
It's a messy business . . . politics. (*Pause.*) Didnay feel
very revolutionary. (*Beat.*) It felt like something . . . but
I dinnay ken if it was revolution. (*Pause.*) Doesnay even
feel real.

Pause.

Gary It doesnay mean anything.

Eddie Aye well . . . I've done it.

Pause.

Gary It's just murder.

Eddie I've made my bones.

Pause.

Gary He was right.

Eddie Good for him.

Gary It means nothing. No one'll notice.

Eddie Good. (*Pause.*) More tay the point . . . (*indicating Tom*) what about that cunt?

Gary (*looks at Tom*) Aye. (*Pause.*) We better get him tay hospital.

Eddie (*to Gary*) You're fucking joking.

Gary No. (*Pause.*) What else can we day?

Eddie (*laughs*) What else can we fucking day?

Gary Aye?

Eddie Get rid ay the cunt.

Gary He's done nothing.

Eddie He'll grass.

Gary He won't.

Eddie (*to Tom*) Aye he fucking will.

Gary He won't. (*Pause.*) I promise.

Eddie You fucking promise.

Gary He's young. (*Beat.*) He'll come round tay our way ay thinking.

   Pause.

Eddie Our way ay fucking thinking? (*Beat.*) Fuck's sake. (*Beat.*) Is there something you're no getting here? (*Beat.*) Our way ay fucking thinking? It's your way ay fucking thinking.

Gary He's no the enemy.

Eddie And (*indicating Frank*) neither was that cunt. And neither's any cunt. (*Beat.*) It's your way ay fucking thinking and it's a lot ay fucking shite. (*Beat.*) So get it intay that fucking skull ay yours . . . there's nothing tay fight against and this shite's fucking over.

Gary It was your idea.

Eddie No . . . I just provided the will.

Gary But you said . . .

Eddie Aye. I said a lot ay fucking things. (*Beat.*) Take a fucking look at yourself. (*Beat.*) You come in here tonight. (*Beat.*) In that stupid coat. (*Laughs.*) You fucking clown. (*Pause.*) What the fuck did you think was gonnay happen?

   Pause.

Gary What would you day if you were me?

   Pause.

Eddie Aye . . . well . . . thank fuck I'm no you.

Gary lunges for Eddie. They struggle for the knife. Eddie gets the better of Gary and holds the knife to his throat.

Aye, you think you're a hard cunt ay. (*Beat.*) But you're fuck all.

Gary tries to struggle free of Eddie. Eddie presses the knife into the flesh on Gary's neck.

You think I won't fucking kill you tay?

Gary stops struggling.

Let me fucking go. (*Pause.*) Let fucking go.

Gary releases his grip on Eddie.

(*Pushes Gary away.*) That cunt (*indicating Frank*) was right . . . you're too fucking emotionally involved. (*Stabs Tom.*) You get attached tay things. (*Stabs Tom.*) That's a big fucking weakness. (*Stabs Tom.*) You end up relying on cunts. (*Stabs Tom.*) This cunt couldnay be relied on. (*Stabs Tom.*) You get rid of everything you cannay rely on. (*Stabs Tom.*) Everything. (*Pause. Moves to stand over Gary.*) I can rely on you ay? (*Beat.*) I need to know. (*Beat.*) You gonnay let me down?

Pause.

Gary What am I gonnay day?

Eddie We're gonnay get out ay here. (*Pause.*) We'll hay tay clean this shit up. (*Beat.*) Get rid ay the bodies. (*Beat.*) We'll put them in the van. Take them down the road. Chuck them in the fucking Forth. (*Beat.*) It'll be like it never fucking happened. (*Beat.*) A disappearance. Simple. Things disappear all the fucking time. Nobody bothers. (*Beat.*) A mystery like . . . but everyone'll soon forget. (*Beat.*) Forgetting's easy. You dinnay even ken you're daying it.

Pause.

Gary What am I gonnay day?

Eddie Day what I day. (*Beat.*) Keep your mouth shut.
Forget about it. It's over.

Pause.

Gary What if I cannay? Like a child

Eddie You have tay. (*Beat.*) It's your only chance.

Pause.

Gary What if I cannay?

Eddie How the fuck can't you?

Pause.

Gary I . . . I havenay . . . I havenay got . . . anything else.

Pause.

Eddie You've got your health. (*Pause. Looks at his
watch.*) We better get a move on. We've got tay be back
in here in two hours. We dinnay want tay be fucking late.

Curtain.